The Nations

The Nations

C.B. Peter Morgan

Destiny Image Publishers
P.O. Box 310
Shippensburg, PA 17257-0310

"We Publish the Prophets"

ISBN 1-56043-090-7

For Worldwide Distribution
Printed in the U.S.A.

Edited by: Bob Buchanan

Contents

Acknowledgments

To God My Father, Creator of the world of nations, who daily teaches me to bear this burden and share His love as He steadily accomplishes His work among the nations.

To Jesus Christ, my constant Friend, Example, Mentor and Big Brother, who urges me to follow Him in this impelling task of establishing the Kingdom of God.

To the Holy Spirit, Comforter and Empowerer, who both reveals God's purpose and destiny and thrusts me forward in a collaborative work of salvation with Him in the world.

To my wife and partner, Pat, with whom I seek to co-labor with God in the development of my nation and who is herself a mother in our nation.

To my children Cathy, Colin, Carrington and Christopher, who have sacrificed much, to whom I trust I will one day present a better Jamaica and who have learned much from my own battle for my people and who will themselves exceed me in their determination to be the salt and substance of their nation.

To the elders, pastors and members of my flock, the Covenant Community Churches, from whom I have learned much and with whom the battle for our nation is being fought and won.

To my Third World colleagues Seth Anyomi, Mensa Otabil, Myles Munroe, Frank Seebransingh, Kingsley Fletcher, Turnel Nelson, Bertril Baird and John Smith, with whose partnership I endeavor to forge new pathways, produce leadership for our people and present to God nations built on Godly principles and ripe for evangelization.

About the Author

Rev. Peter Morgan, a Jamaican, is senior pastor of the Covenant Community Churches of Jamaica, a founding director of the Deeper Life Ministries, the Institute for National Reconstruction and the Covenant Christian Academy, and one of the foremost Christian leaders of the Third World nations. He has ministered extensively in many countries of the world and as a historian by training has closely followed the hand and move of God in nations. He is married to Patricia, a Trinidadian, university educator at Oral Roberts University and author of *The Battle for the Seed*. They have four children for whom they labor to provide the inheritance of a better Jamaica.

Peter is a statesman and intercessor who stands in the gap for the nations. His pilgrimage in carrying a nine foot cross throughout Jamaica impels him to turn the heart of God to his nation and the heart of his nation back to God.

Foreword

The world's population has more than doubled in the past three decades from 2.5 billion in 1950 to 5 billion in 1988. On the United Nation's medium growth assumption, the population is expected to reach 6.2 billion by the end of the century and 8.5 billion by the year 2025.

The present population of 5 billion make their homes in the more than 170 nations that comprise our planet Earth today. This is the world of which we all are a part. We belong to the family of man and are all brothers, sharing one common heritage in creation. In essence, we are the world.

When I was a child there was a song we learned in Sunday school with words that stated: "Take this whole world but give me Jesus" and "The world behind me, the cross before." This song sums up the attitude of the religious communities toward the world in general. However, I discovered a problem when I read with understanding for the first time the well-known passage of

Scripture: "For God so loved the world, that He gave His only begotten Son...." (John 3:16, KJV). Suddenly it struck me that it did not say, "for God so loved the church or the righteous." It is the world He loves. Is it possible that we in our quest, based on misguided perception, have abandoned and turned our backs on the very thing we were supposed to love? Much of our Christian theology has equated the "spirit of the world" with the world and the earth. We have perceived the "nation" to be of satanic origin and a tool of his device and therefore should be shunned, alienated and condemned to destruction. From this theological premise was developed the mentality and religious position that prepares the individual to escape the "world" and abandon the earth for Heaven.

However, a closer look at the Scriptures reveals a totally different perspective on the origin, purpose and future of the nations of the world. In Acts 17:26 we find some very powerful words: "From one man He made every nation of men...and He determined the times set for them and the exact places where they should live." Here we see the fact that the nations were created by God for a specific purpose and therefore are essential to His objectives. Jesus, in His final instructions to His disciples, commanded them to "Go and make disciples of all *nations*." He also stated that in the final judgment, He will gather the "nations" and judge among them. He also promised Abraham that He would make him the father of a great nation and that his seed would bless the nations of the world. God has definitely included the salvation of the nation in His primary plan.

He also seems to have designed the Church to preserve the nation and secure the citizens for the Kingdom of God.

I believe that the pages of the book you are about to read is one of the most important documents written in recent times. C.B. Peter Morgan presents one of the most vital, well-researched and practical insights into the role of the nation in God's original plan and into the relationship of the Church to the nation. He also, in a thoughtful and thought-provoking manner, illuminates the subject and engages you to consider your personal responsibility for the welfare of your own nation. At a time when governments, politicians, civic agencies and all of our institutions seem to be without direction and a sense of purpose, the need to rediscover and redefine the purpose and function of this vital human corporate entity is a must. Peter Morgan, in this inspiring, insightful, captivating and wise exposition, provides us with a fresh vision for the future of the nations and sets out the ingredients necessary for reclaiming and restoring our national destinies. Every serious student of political science, education and social sciences would do well to make this book a required text in his pursuit of knowledge of how a nation works. Government officials and all those involved in the formation and development of public policy should heed the solid, practical guidance that this philosophically rich volume contains.

It is my earnest desire that you read this work carefully and allow the Creator of nations to rekindle in your heart the burden that is in His heart for the salvation and discipling of your nation and the nations of the world.

"Where there is no vision or revelation, the people perish."

Dr. Myles Munroe
Nassau, Bahamas

Preface

As a young Christian I spent much of my time studying the Church. I had little concern trying to understand the world "God so loved."

This book will be better appreciated if we defined the biblical concept "world" from which nations are derived.

Five common terms for "world" are used in the Scriptures:

(1) *Ge* is the earth, ground, land, the terrestrial sphere as different from heaven (e.g. Rev. 13:3; Matt. 5:13, 18; Jer. 10:11; 25:26).

(2) *Oikoumene* is the world of peoples, the inhabitants of the earth (e.g. Acts 17:31; Ps. 33:8; Is. 34:1-2).

(3) *Aion* is an age, an epoch, a period of time. The age of man is marked by moral and spiritual decadence. Hence its cares (Matt. 13:22) its wisdom

(1 Cor. 1:20; 2:6; 3:18) its fashion (Rom. 12:2) its gods (2 Cor. 4:4) its rulers (1 Cor. 2:6,8) are all under the judgment of God and will come to an end (1 Cor. 3:18; Eph. 2:2).

(4) The most frequently used term is *kosmos*. It is applied variously as follows:

(a) The entire expanse of the created universe (the cosmos) structured with systematic order, harmony and artistic beauty (Acts 17:24; Rom. 1:20; Ps. 104).

(b) The temporal possessions (Matt. 16:26) derived from the material resources of the earth, sea and air (Gen. 2:12).

(c) The human race, mankind (e.g. Matt. 5:14; Jonn 1:9,10; John 3:16,17,19).

(d) The present moral and spiritual condition of human affairs in alienation from and opposition to God (John 8:23; 1 John 2:15-17). This is characterized as being under the influence of the "prince of the world" (John 14:30), the "spirit of this world" (1 Cor. 2:12), and the presence of the antichrist (1 John 4:5).

The Old Testament has no one word for the spatial/temporal world but uses such all-inclusive terms as "the heavens, even the highest heavens, and all their starry host, the earth and all that is on it, the seas and all that is in them" (Neh. 9:6; Ex. 20:11).

The Hebrew mind thinks wholistically, hence no one term is isolated in its use. One is inclusive of others. This is as much true in referring to the "world" as it is true of the term "nation" in this book.

Introduction

The world seems to be a chaotic place at times. Nations and kingdoms rise and fall. Economies soar and crumble. Armies advance and retreat. The confusion of our world and national systems may cause some to believe that history is proceeding along at random, with neither design nor purpose. Not long ago, I read "the back of the Book" once again! There I found that God had recorded a glimpse of His plan. The final pages of the Bible show us a wonderful destiny that human history is rushing toward.

> *And I heard a loud voice from the throne saying, "**Now the dwelling of God is with men, and He will live with them.** They will be His people and God Himself will be with them and be their God. He will wipe every tear from their eyes. There will be no more death or mourning or crying or pain, for the old order of things has passed away."*
>
> Revelation 21:3-4

I did not see a temple in the city, because the Lord God Almighty and the Lamb are its temple. The city does not need the sun or the moon to shine on it, for the glory of God gives it light, and the kings of the earth will bring their splendor into it. On no day will its gates ever be shut, for there will be no night there. The glory and honor of the nations will be brought into it. Nothing impure will ever enter it, nor will anyone who does what is shameful or deceitful, but only those whose names are written in the Lamb's book of life.

Revelation 21:22-27

God's ultimate destiny for humankind is glorious to think about. It is His deep abiding desire to come down and dwell among men. We can't begin to imagine how wonderful the day will be when we live and rule with Him forever. However, we haven't entered our final reign yet. God has some plans yet to fulfill. I invite you to join me as we study God's purpose for the nations and discover a part of His marvelous plan to use His Church to close human history as we know it.

Chapter One

The Origin of Nations

"God so loved the world" (John 3:16). God's eyes are not as much on the Church as they are on the world. It took me a long time to be convinced about this because I was taught that I should not love the world. How can God love the world, and I can't?

We need to understand the use of the word "world." The psalmist wrote, "The earth is the Lord's and everything in it, the world and all who live in it" (Psalm 24:1). When God made the world He said, "That's good." Everything He made was useful to fulfill the purpose for which it was created. The world He made consists of the earth, its resources, its governmental systems and structures and its people. The world God made was corrupted by sin. Adam's disobedience set in place a demonic agency with its principles and influences contrary to the will and purpose of God and establishing darkness over God's creation.

1

However, God's mandate given to Adam and Eve in Genesis 1:26-28 was not revoked. God's plan to redeem the whole world was immediately established in Genesis 3, verse 15: "And I will put enmity between you and the woman, and between your offspring and hers; he will crush your head, and you will strike his heel." God is a God of order. To carry out His purpose, God structured the world of His creation into nations.

Paul explains the origin of nations in his sermon at Athens, recorded in Acts chapter seventeen.

> *The God who made the world and everything in it is the Lord of heaven and earth and does not live in temples built by hands, as if He needed anything, because He Himself gives all men life and breath and everything else. From one man He made every nation of men, that they should inhabit the whole earth, and He determined the times set for them and the exact places where they should live.*
>
> Acts 17:24-26

What Is a Nation?

Webster's Dictionary defines a nation as "A stable, historically developed community of people with a territory, economic life, distinctive culture, and language in common...united under a single government." Simply stated, a nation could be described as a large group of people who share certain things in common.

What we first think of when we consider "nation" is, its land with its natural resources. The land is geographically designed and given a name which identifies the nation. People have common ethnic characteristics,

2

common origins and historic experiences which bind them together.

A nation shares a common group of mores and behaviors, written laws and oral traditions. One nation may consider murder the ultimate crime against her citizens. Another, from a less civilized background, may consider the murder of an unsuspecting victim an act of great honor. Nations usually share both formal and informal structures. Everything from systems of entertainment to economics and architecture are a part of what may be identified as the culture of a particular nation.

Nations also share a common government. At one time most nations were governed by kings and dictators. The citizens identified with the ruler. They were loyal to the throne and prayed for the continuation of the reign of the monarch. Today, a variety of governments exists. Some nations elect a parliament or congress. Others are ruled by oligarchies from a particular political party or military command. Regardless of the form it takes, sharing a common government is part of the definition of a nation. One cannot be a true citizen of one nation and be loyal to the government of another.

God's Hand in Nation-building

The most important element of a nation is its people. The land alone is not the nation. The culture or government is not the nation. Nations are people. All the people of all nations came from one man. God created Adam. From Adam all of the people of the nations were born.

We have such an exalted view of mankind that we think human effort devised the nations. We may think that a common land, language, government or social structure is what brought people together to form a nation. Scriptures indicate that much more planning is involved in the formation of nations than random human effort.

God chooses, in His Sovereignty, where we live and what nation we will be a part of. God takes an active role in humanity's history. I had not always understood how God was involved in the history of the nations. As a new Christian, young in the Lord, I had nations described to me as something "worldly" and under the control of the devil. We were mostly interested in discussing the rapture and the return of Christ. While we praised and prayed, our focus was so high in the clouds that we couldn't see what God was really doing here on earth. God's plan includes far more than simply waiting to meet Him in the sky. I had my bags packed and I was ready to go. The worse the nation became, and the farther into sin the people fell, the more convinced we became that Christ's coming was near. I have learned since those early days that nations are not formed by politicians, explorers or scientists. God established nations. He seeded the nations through Adam. The nations originated from divine initiatives found in the first three chapters of the Bible.

This is the account of the heavens and the earth when they were created. When the Lord God made the earth and the heavens...The Lord God formed the man from the dust of the ground and breathed into his nostrils the breath of life, and the man became a living being... The Lord God took the man and put him in the Garden of Eden to work it and take care of it... The Lord God said it is not good for the man to be alone. I will make a helper suitable for him... So the Lord God caused the man to fall into a deep sleep, and while he was sleeping He took one of the man's ribs and closed up the place with flesh. Then the Lord God made a woman from the rib He had taken out of the man, and He brought her to the man.

Genesis 2:4,7,15,18,21-22

We must realize that God was after something bigger than just Adam. He had a plan for Adam, so He gave him the responsibility and the tools to till the garden. God had more in store for him than just being a gardener. God gave Adam a wife.

God blessed them and said to them, "Be fruitful and increase in number, fill the earth and subdue it. Rule over the fish of the sea and the birds of the air and every living creature that moves on the ground."

Genesis 1:28

In the Caribbean Islands each family has a little fence around their parcel of land. I imagine that is much the way Adam saw things. His garden was a manageable, geographic region. Surely it would have been overwhelming for him to have handled far beyond that by himself. God commanded Adam and Eve to multiply. That is exactly what humanity has done. Adam kept the garden and began to raise a family. Little did he know that he and Eve were destined to be the parents of hundreds of nations. That was the destiny of his seed.

Mankind multiplied quickly. It took only a short time for families to be born. Within only a few generations people had begun to group families into tribes and small communities developed. Jabal became "the father of those who live in tents and raise livestock" (Genesis 4:20). The tribe of Jubal were musicians. They developed skill at playing the harp and flute. Tubal-Cain's tribe began to work bronze and iron. They were a tribe of industrialists.

After the flood of Noah's day, instinctively mankind again quickly organized into clans and tribes. Javan became the father of maritime people who set out to sea, and Nimrod became a mighty warrior. Civilizations developed into nations about this time, as can be evidenced by the population center in ancient Babylonia and the empire which developed under Nimrod the king.

> *Cush was the father of Nimrod who grew up to be a mighty warrior on the earth. He was a mighty hunter before the Lord; that is why it is said, "Like Nimrod, a mighty hunter before the Lord." The first centers of his kingdom were Babylon, Erech, and Calneh in Shinar. From that land he went to Assyria where he built Nineveh and Calah; that is the great city.*
>
> Genesis 10:8-12

Noah had three sons: Shem, Ham and Japheth. All the nations of the earth came from Adam through Noah. Therefore, these three sons laid the foundation for all of the people groups which exist today. The tribal group which grew from Japheth's seed moved northward and settled in regions around the Black and Caspian seas.

Their descendants became the caucasian races of Europe and Asia, including the natives of North America who probably crossed the Berring Straits from Asia and moved southward to warmer climates in the western hemisphere.

The clans and tribes from the seed of Ham moved southward. The names given Ham's descendants are similar to those of land areas in central Arabia, Egypt, the east shore of the Mediterranean Sea and the eastern coast of Africa. Interestingly, Egypt was once called "the land of Ham" and the name of an early pagan god of Egypt was a transliteration of the name Ham. This has led some to believe that Ham led the migration into Egypt. Nimrod was also a descendant of Ham.

Shem's descendants stayed closer to the Middle East and made up the central nations of the eastern hemisphere. The Bible gives us the genealogy from Shem to Abraham, the father of the Jews. Most of those who are fighting in the Middle East in modern times are truly all members of the Semitic tribes. Arabs and Israelis are both Semites. Arabic nations have sprung from Abraham's son Ishmael while Israel consists of descendants of Abraham through Isaac and Jacob.

Nations are people groups who hold certain things in common. Some nations are great and powerful while others are less dominant. Regardless of the stature, God has instituted the nations. Today when God establishes a nation, He may cause a people to come together from different traditions, different languages, different cultures; but He weaves them together as one integrated community. They have common problems, common difficulties, common hopes and aspirations. So He organizes the world into nations.

The Seeds of God's Purpose

The first five books of the Bible show the seeds of God's purpose in the development of the nations. He starts with ethnic consciousness from the perspective of the family and family relationships. Ethnicity is important in establishing personal identity and the sense of belonging in any people. At this point government is vested in paternalistic leadership, much like Abraham's. Next, He allows them to develop a social contract with central community leadership, as exemplified by Moses and the elders of Israel governing the people under the laws and statutes of the covenant of God. It is here in the wilderness that God teaches the people to acknowledge the inalienable God-given rights of the individual. To respect these rights is to strengthen the corporate bond of the covenanted community.

The establishment of a nation demands identification with its own land. Canaan was given to a people who were coming of age so that they could responsibly exercise the dominion mandate God gave to them to be stewards of the earth. As nations develop, it is God who structures them into governmental institutions organized with systems within a common geo-political sphere. Definitively, a nation is not a nation unless it remains a nation under God!

Nations are no accident. The Bible proves there is a master plan that is not merely in the hands of governments and powerful men. People have been brought together according to God's purposes. He has a destiny for the nations. God's purposes cannot be diminished by the pride, arrogance and sin of humanity. He is Sovereign. The psalmist sang, "O Lord God Almighty, who is like You? You are mighty, O Lord, and Your faithfulness surrounds You" (Psalm 89:8).

Does your nation truly understand why God brought its people together? There are many reasons given by politicians, sociologists and economists. In the Caribbean for example, God brought people together all the way from Africa and India, Europe and the Middle East for His purpose.

The discovery of God's purpose and destiny for the nations is one of the most wonderful discoveries you will ever make. The challenge and the reward of being the people He wants us to be is beyond comprehension at times. Don't believe those who would say that you have to keep your faith separate from your national life. The enemy would love for Christians to think that mankind is in control and the nations must run their own courses. If the devil can convince believers to abandon the nation, then he can continue to infiltrate and bring confusion in the world. Man is not in control of his destiny—God is!

Join me now as we look at how God has given destiny to the nations, and how He causes human events to fulfill His purposes.

Chapter Two

Preserving the Purpose and Destiny of Nations

The Condition of the World

Great gatherings of people come together in different parts of the world at different times. Parliaments meet to decide the fate of nations. Business leaders and economists meet to determine the financial direction of great corporations. Thousands gather to be entertained by great sportsmen, musicians and actors. Scientists and educators confer to deliberate and record their greatest findings.

Regardless of the schemes of humanity, there is no gathering upon the face of the earth that is potentially more significant than the gathering of the people of the living God. In God's people are locked up the hope, purpose and destiny of the nations

Yet, there is a world of persons who are cringing and wringing its hands in despair. So many are filled with fear. Men and women are strutting about the streets and congregating on the corners, puncturing their veins with drugs and filling up their bodies with the wine that dissipates and destroys. There are those in the dark cities who are planning and scheming to rob their brothers and sisters who are more privileged than they are.

What a shame that the greatest cause of death among youth in our western culture is suicide! Many waste away slowly with the poison of misplaced values and self-gratification.

Great nations have come together, at the end of themselves to know how to make their economy work. Others meet to evaluate emergency plans that deal with every kind of natural disaster and environmental dilemma imaginable. Direction, purpose and destiny seem to get lost in a world where morals are polluted and values are given over to the practice of the atheistic and supersititous occult.

The face of the map is constantly changing, as sources of governmental power become more difficult than ever to determine. Governments must reevaluate their condition constantly in this ever-changing world in which we live. Allegiances to empires are being realigned. Those who thought they could never fall have fallen.

All in all, we live in a world that has been going headlong on a slippery road to reprobation. Judgment ominously hangs over the world in which we live.

The condition of the world is a tragedy, but it is no surprise. It was described long ago in prophecy. It is already determined that nations in the world under the kingdom of darkness will come to shattering destruction because of the judgment that is upon it. Does the following describe your nation?

The merchants of the earth will weep and mourn over her because no one buys their cargoes any more—cargoes of gold, silver, precious stones and pearls; fine linen, purple silk and scarlet cloth; every sort of citron wood, and articles of every kind made of ivory, costly wood, bronze, iron, and marble; cargoes of cinnamon and spice, of incense, myrrh, and frankincense, of wine and olive oil, of fine flour and wheat; cattle and sheep; horses and carriages; and bodies and souls of men. They will say, "The fruit you longed for is gone from you. All your riches and splendor have vanished, never to be recovered." The merchants who sold these things and gained their wealth from her will stand far off, terrified at her torment. They will weep and mourn.

Revelation 18:11-15

A World without Purpose

The conditions described in that scripture are the result of man's vain attempts to design political and social economies without God. The result is national collapse under God's judgment. There is a greater tragedy in the midst of this chaotic world, however. It is the tragedy of the people of God not understanding their destiny and purpose as believers. The world is clouded by sin and therefore obviously misses God's intention.

"There is a way that seems right to a man, but in the end it leads to death" (Proverbs 14:12).

The truth is that the people of the world will remain tragically condemned if the people who have been called from out of the world do not understand their purpose. I'm talking about the Church of Jesus Christ.

Thanks be to God that through the eyes of faith we can look past the destruction, distress and despair of the world and see a vision of hope. We see, rising up from the cultural waste of humanity, a new generation with a counter-culture. There is a generation that has found God. This is a generation with purpose and with a sense of destiny, a new generation.

The End Precedes the Beginning

What is purpose? Purpose is the reason for a thing. It answers the question "Why?" It describes the intention in the mind of the Creator. Whatever is made is equipped to function according to the purpose for which the thing was created.

What is destiny? Destiny is the vision of a completed purpose. In God's mind, the end precedes the beginning. In other words, destiny is tied to purpose. We cannot speak of the purpose of a nation unless we tie it to the destiny of that nation.

Whatever God plans for man was ordained from the beginning. The history of any people is tied to God's purpose for that people. The plans of any nation are futile and will come to naught unless they are aligned to

God's destiny for that nation. Unfortunately, not every nation finds God's plan.

A few years ago I worked for the government of my country. We would gather together and organize our plans. The government wanted ten-year plans. Long-range planning is definitely beneficial. It is hard to get anywhere if you don't know where you are going. Planning gives you direction. It helps you to have purpose and to measure the success of your time, energy and resources. It helps you to know whether you are remaining on track, according to the plan. However, we must remember that plans made outside the will of God are a waste of time. "Many are the plans in a man's heart, but it is the Lord's purpose that prevails" (Proverbs 19:21).

Adolf Hitler had a tremendous plan. His strategy was brilliant. In his plan, the Third Reich of Germany would endure for one hundred years. Hitler's government didn't last for five years. Mao Tse Tung doubled his fist before Almighty God and swore that he would replace the religion of God with the religion of man. Now they can't find his bones and a revival of the religion of God is breaking out in Mao's China. It is God who determines the course of a nation's history.

God is indeed Sovereign. In order to better understand His Sovereignty over authorities and rulers, let us take a journey through history to find out how His Sovereignty has been displayed in the past. A review of what He has done before will help us to understand His purpose and destiny for the nations.

We have shown that God made the whole earth and that things went wrong. God never intended that the world should function without His involvement. He made the earth. He made the world, but He placed man there to be the stewards and the governors of the earth. Mankind was given dominion. "God blessed them and said to them, 'Be fruitful and increase in number, fill the earth and subdue it. Rule over the fish of the sea and the birds of the air and every living creature that moves on the ground' " (Genesis 1:28).

Man's ability to govern the earth quickly became flawed because of sin. Man sold himself out to God's enemy. However, the command to have dominion never changed, so mankind still has the same mandate. But he now has the wrong master. He's now functioning in obedience to his new master. Satan's intentions are to systematically destroy God's world. Humanity has been misusing the principle of dominion over everything on the earth ever since. Satan is wreaking havoc over the earth and its resources within governments and among the people. He has been using sinful men to abuse the principle of dominion over all of God's creation.

Intervention by Flood

At one point in history God looked down from Heaven. He saw the horrible condition of man. There was not one righteous man, not even one. Every imagination of the hearts of men was evil continually. God repented that He ever made man. Now that's the hardest word that could ever come upon any child or upon any creature. Did your parents ever say to you, "I'm sorry for the day you were born?" That's tough!

God was sorry that He made man. Man had thrown off God's government and superimposed his own self-government. His willful acts led to rebellion and anarchy. It grieved God because of what was happening, but He didn't give up on man. God so loved the world He had created that He developed a plan to intervene in human history. His plan was a plan of judgment and of grace.

> *So the Lord said, "I will wipe mankind whom I have created, from the face of the earth—men and animals and creatures that move along the ground, and birds of the air—for I am grieved that I have made them." But Noah found favor in the eyes of the Lord...Now the earth was corrupt in God's sight and was full of violence...So God said to Noah... "Make yourself an ark of cypress wood...I am going to bring flood waters on the earth to destroy all life under the heavens...But I will establish my covenant with you."*
>
> Genesis 6:5-8,11,14,18

A high level of corruption, selfish exploitation and rapacious greed pervades our modern societies. Envy, hatred and violence so threaten the security of the community, I wonder whether we could survive a visitation from God to our cities.

God gave Noah specific instructions concerning the construction of an ark. It was to be a sanctuary that would provide safety for a righteous remnant while the remainder of life would be destroyed. God wanted to redeem mankind. Only one family found favor. Noah, his wife and his children were allowed to be preserved in the ark. God saw in this man a patriarch that would collaborate with Him in the re-establishment of righteousness based on God's principles.

God's plan called for the ark to be about 450 feet long, 75 feet wide and 45 feet high. It must have been comparable to a modern ship. No one could be more aware of the balance of nature than God. He commanded Noah to take pairs of animals with him into the ark. It was God's plan of intervention to preserve His creatures.

God again intervened in human history. Had mankind continued at the rate of wickedness and destruction God found in Noah's day, the race would have become extinct. But God had an eternal purpose. His love for the world and His creation caused Him to extinguish the type of threat which brought sin and death and to preserve mankind through the family of Noah, as well as animal life. Noah had little idea that his destiny would be pivotal in the plan of God for mankind and His renewed planet. God knows what He is doing. When the schemes of men rush headlong toward destruction, God knows how to interrupt man's plans and preserve His intention to redeem the world.

Intervention by Dispersion

Some years later God was again discerning the course of the nations. He peered down to see what a new generation was doing. As the nations proliferated, they migrated across the face of the earth to fulfill God's purpose. However, they began to build a civilization unto themselves. They established an empire in Babylonia which included walled cities with soaring towers.

Now the world had one language and a common speech. As men moved eastward, they found a plain in Shinar and settled there. They said to each other, "Come let's make bricks and bake them thoroughly." They used bricks instead of stone, and tar for mortar. Then they said, "Come, let us build ourselves a city with a tower that reaches to the heavens, so that we may make a name for ourselves and not be scattered over the face of the whole earth."

Genesis 11:1-4

I want you to understand what is happening. As a civilization developed into large cities, walls with observation towers became common. However, this tower in the plain of Shinar, often referred to as the Tower of Babel, was more than simply an observation tower. This tower was one which would allow men to reach heaven. They weren't interested in the true God or in the pure way of faith which would enable them to reach heaven. This tower was devoted to pagan worship of many gods. This was probably a temple-tower known as a ziggurat. It was quite wide at the bottom and consisted of increasingly smaller levels. It resembled a stairway into the sky. The base of the tower was surrounded with chapels devoted to the various gods worshiped at the time.

Not only were the people devoted to the practice of paganism, they were also full of human pride. You may recall that it was satan's pride which originally caused

19

him to rebel against God and lead the revolt which led to his expulsion from Heaven. Here mankind is filled with pride and arrogance. God is certainly opposed to such an attitude. "To fear the Lord is to hate evil; I hate pride and arrogance, evil behavior and perverse speech" (Proverbs 8:13).

The potential for human accomplishment is beyond our imagination. However, our God-given potential should not arrogate itself to a position of pride. Seeing that the direction of mankind was toward proud paganism and that they were united in their opposition against God by building the tower, God decided once again to intervene in human history.

Mankind had devised a plan. God had a different idea for that nation. The last major intervention in history had resulted in the destruction of the earth by water. God had something different for the people at Shinar.

> *But the Lord came down to see the city and the tower that the men were building. The Lord said, "If as one people speaking the same language they have begun to do this, then nothing they plan to do will be impossible for them. Come let Us go down and confuse their language so they will not understand each other." So the Lord scattered them from there over all the earth, and they stopped building the city.*
>
> Genesis 11:5-8

We often become comfortable and complacent in our positions or locations. We tend to like familiar surroundings. God wanted man to fill the earth. Centralized, autonomous man always seeks to deify his selfish ambitions and idolize his humanistic achievements. God confounded the languages of the people at Babel in order to stop the united tendency toward paganism and to force human beings to spread out over the surface of the planet. We are created for God's purposes. He manipulates the nations to meet those ends.

Intervention by Fire

Another example of God's sovereign hand in history is found in Genesis, chapters eighteen and nineteen. It is the story of Sodom and Gomorrah. Lot and his family were in Sodom. The city had become immoral and the people had become sexually perverted and fiercely violent. It had lost its community spirit. God's judgment was coming upon the nation. The following passage describes the state of the nation, God's impending judgment and the intercessory cry of one righteous leader.

> *Then the Lord said, "The outcry against Sodom and Gomorrah is so great and their sin is so grievous that I will go down and see if what they have done is as bad as the outcry that has reached me. If not, I will know." The men turned away and went toward Sodom but Abraham remained standing before the Lord. Then Abraham approached Him and said, "Will You sweep away the righteous with the wicked? What if there are fifty righteous people in the city? Will You really sweep it away and not spare the place for the sake of the fifty righteous people in it?"*

> Genesis 18:20-24

God destroys nations. Here Abraham is praying and interceding on behalf of Sodom. He said, "Lord, surely

You wouldn't destroy the righteous with the wicked. How can You destroy the nation?" It's always good to challenge God by His own Word. "Suppose I can find fifty; would You save the nation?" He says OK. "Let that be forty-five, Lord." OK. "Forty." "Twenty." Down to ten. In the end God destroyed Sodom and Gomorrah. Would God really have saved Sodom? Absolutely! God is true to His word. He promised that He would have spared the place for as few as ten righteous people. However, the angels' visit to Sodom only confirmed that the city deserved destruction.

Lot saw the angels and had enough insight to recognize that they were holy. They planned to spend the night in the town square. However, Lot would not allow them to do so.

> *But he insisted so strongly that they did go with him and entered his house. He prepared a meal for them baking bread without yeast, and they ate. Before they had gone to bed, all the men from every part of the city of Sodom—both young and old—surrounded the house. They called to Lot, "Where are the men who came to you tonight? Bring them out to us so that we can have sex with them."*
>
> Genesis 19:3-5

This event only served to show the depravity of the citizens. God's hand of wrath was lifted in judgment upon the two cities. You can read how God caused fire and burning sulfur to rain on the cities of Sodom and Gomorrah and destroyed the inhabitants. Sodom and Gomorrah had reached a point of no return.

The creeping moral degeneracy of our people is leading to a progressive dehumanization of our generation. Permissive sexual promiscuity is giving way to every form of sexual perversion. Personal ungodliness is now so conventional it is becoming culturally, institutionally and legally oppressive. Has your city reached the point of no return? Sodom and Gomorrah had become so defiled that God wanted to prevent them from polluting the rest of the world. He intervened in human history and destroyed those cities where He could find not even ten righteous people.

One important "modus operandi" of God stands out. God has always preserved a remnant. During Noah's day God brought a flood, yet preserved life through the ark. At Babel God caused men to scatter and stopped the building of the temple-tower by confusing their languages. Then He called Abram. Sodom and Gomorrah were destroyed with burning sulfur, although Lot and his daughters were spared. God has a strong and purposeful interest in preserving mankind. He has a plan, a purpose and a destiny for the nations.

Intervention by Prophetic Proclamation

Some might argue that God intervened in these instances among His chosen people to preserve the lineage for the birth of the Messiah. However, there are many examples of how He has moved among Gentile nations which have no connection to the biological lineage of Jesus. Perhaps the greatest story of how He intervened among Gentiles is found in the Book of Jonah. In this case, God's intervention was not one of judgment unto destruction, but one of mercy unto salvation

Jonah was a prophet of God in Israel. He was instructed to go to the Assyrian capitol of Nineveh and warn the residents that God would soon destroy their city, and thus destroy their nation. Jonah did not want to take such a message to this city.

The Assyrians had already conquered Damascus and were a tremendous threat to Israel. How could he preach to the enemy? Was he afraid that they would believe his message and repent?

Jonah wanted God to destroy Nineveh. Perhaps he went to a group just like some of our modern churches and asked whether he should go. He did not think God would want a Jew to go and preach to Gentiles about the God of Israel. He tried to excuse himself with every kind of human reasoning possible. Eventually he took a boat in the opposite direction of Nineveh. Through circumstances that were not entirely within his own control, he was swallowed by a giant fish which emptied him on the shore near Nineveh. It was certainly a roundabout way to get to where God wanted him to be. The following passage reveals God's desire to use Jonah as the instrument through which He could change the course of a nation.

On the first day, Jonah started into the city. He proclaimed: "Forty more days and Nineveh will be overturned." The Ninevites believed God. They declared a fast, and all of them, from the greatest to the least, put on sackcloth. When the news reached the king of Nineveh, he rose from his throne, covered himself with sackcloth and sat down in the dust. Then he issued a

*proclamation in Nineveh: "Do not let any man or beast,
herd or flock, taste anything; do not let them eat or
drink. But let man and beast be covered with sackcloth.
Let everyone call urgently on God. Let them give up
their evil ways and their violence. Who knows? God
may yet relent and with compassion turn from his fierce
anger so that we will not perish." When God saw what
they did and how they turned from their evil ways, He
had compassion and did not bring upon them the
destruction He had threatened.*

Jonah 3:4-10

That had to be one tremendous revival meeting.
There could have been as many as 600,000 people in the
city when Jonah preached. God had made him a very
convincing prophet. Even the government yielded to
God. Yet Jonah was disappointed. He had only reluctant-
ly preached the message, and when the people repented
he was sad. Jonah wanted God to destroy Israel's enemy.

But God asked the recurring and pivotal question,
"Should I not be concerned about that great city?"
(Jonah 4:11b). The city repented and God withheld His
hand of judgment and saved Nineveh. This does not
necessarily mean all the people of Nineveh are in
Heaven, but it does mean that God preserves a nation.
He turns back the hand of judgment and He causes His
people to move into His will, His way. He makes us to walk
in righteousness, sometimes in spite of ourselves. I'm sure
that from then on Jonah must have had tremendous
revivals. His preaching could have brought thousands to
know Jehovah God. God honors repentance.

Establishing Every Nation of Men

The earth belongs to God. Everything that comes from out of the earth belongs to God. The world belongs to God and everybody in it belongs to God. Nations were established by God. Remember that Paul's sermon in Athens said, "From one man he made every nation of men" (Acts 17:26a). The United States of America is established by God. Russia is established by God. Your nation is established by God. The sermon goes on to say that He determines the times and the exact places set for men and nations.

Many years ago the forefathers of those living in the island nations of the Caribbean were torn from their tribes on the shores of Africa. Some came from India as indentured servants. Others migrated from England and from other parts of the world. Whatever the historical circumstances or personal motives, they would be fashioned and molded to form nations of peoples.

This prophet's word spoken in 1978 helps us to reinterpret the history of Jamaica from God's point of view:

This is what God says:

"From the ends of the earth, I brought you; from vast Africa, cold Europe, distant Asia. I tore you from your earth-bound culture, your fetish practices, your superstitious charms, to form a new man with heart and mind and will, not bound to the past, but fixed to a new destiny—OUT OF MANY, ONE PEOPLE.

"I sent My name amongst you, says God. I stamped it on your heart. Through the curse of slavery and the pain of Imperial rule, I was your only freedom—your guiding star. I gave you songs to sing, of hope of better things to come. I left you My Word, your minds to absorb, your hearts to embrace, and your ways to follow. So, you were known across the world as Christians—My People.

"And behold, says God, I watched you from childhood. I nursed your wounds; I established in you, families to heal you of your orphan spirit. I gave you schools, I set up hospitals; I founded clubs and businesses by My hand. Your leaders had visions inspired by My Word—of freedom, respect for all, charity, justice, truth forever; a vision of God's glory in the land. And so, says God, when you hoisted your flag of independence you sang to Me and you called Me Father—and I was glad; for it was I who blessed you with a mighty hand.

"Remember, says God, You did not choose me; I chose you. And yet—you have forgotten Me, says God. Neither have you cared for your own brothers and sisters. Your fetish gods which once were your shame, now you openly consult. With superstitious spirits of your forefathers you again conspire. You create gods of men and you worship them. You call yourself by new names, confusing 'I man,' with I AM. You applaud evil and you honor

27

deceit. You scramble amongst the cultural heaps of the past to find an identity more distant than the new creation that I have formed in you. But all you have trusted have failed and shall never succeed until—until again you call Me Father, eternal to save, who will bless your land by His mighty hand. That I will do, says God, for that is My plan. And when you choose Me, you will recall that I first chose you—OUT OF MANY, ONE PEOPLE."

Most nations possess an innate sense of being birthed by a determined spirit that is bigger than a purely human agency. It is a divine consciousness of destiny often enshrined in anthems, national pledges and constitutions. Whether it is acknowledged as divine or not, history eventually vindicates the sovereign hand of God in the affairs of men.

Whether it is by flood, fire or manipulation of events, God displays His Sovereignty. God is determined to bring a nation to its destiny so that His purpose can be fulfilled. There is no greater example of God working in a nation than that of ancient Israel. Let us look at how God used one man to raise up a nation that would preserve His plan and bring salvation to mankind.

Chapter Three

Israel: God's Chosen Nation

Depravity of Man

An indictment of the entire human race is found in the Book of Romans. The passage proves the need for a Savior because of the sinfulness of mankind. Few can boast concerning human achievement when they recognize the way mankind has fallen from the glory God intended man to have.

For although they knew God, they neither glorified Him as God nor gave thanks to Him, but their thinking became futile and their foolish hearts were darkened. Although they claimed to be wise they became fools and exchanged the glory of the immortal God for images made to look like mortal man and birds and animals and reptiles. Therefore God gave them over in the sinful desires of their hearts to sexual impurity for the degrading of their bodies with one another. They exchanged the truth of God for a lie, and worshipped and served created things rather than the Creator–who is forever praised. Amen.

Romans 1:21-25

This was exactly the condition of the world at the time of Abram. The first people on earth, Adam and Eve, knew God in an intimate way. They could talk with Him in the garden. After they sinned and were cast out of the garden, their children worshiped God by bringing sacrifices. However, as the generations passed, people began to worship other things instead of the one true God. Men developed the worship of many gods. They would shape stone into images and bow in worship to these statues. Often a family, clan or region would have its own patron god.

In order to understand how far noble man had fallen, we can look at some of the religious practices found among Abram's people. Their worship seemed to be connected with nature and the ability of the elements to provide food and to satisfy sensual lust, not unlike the cravings of modern men.

One false god of the day was called Baal. As the sun god, he was seen and worshiped in two different ways. They believed he could warm the earth and help bring forth vegetation. They also believed he could burn the earth and scorch the crop. During times of plague or famine they believed Baal was angry. Therefore they would offer human sacrifice to appease him. This sacrifice was usually the first born of the one making the offering.

Another god worshiped during the period was called Ashtoreth. This is the female counterpart of Baal, often connected with worship of the moon. The Ashtoreth idols were female and often accompanied those of Baal. Worship of this goddess was generally sexual in nature. Her temples were surrounded by prostitutes at times, and worship usually consisted of sexual orgies. This worship was connected with warfare.

The peace-time goddess was known as Asherah. This idol was generally made as statues with many breasts since Asherah was the goddess of love and fertility, often referred to as "groves" in the Old Testament. The Bible frequently condemns the nation of Israel for falling into the worship of this false god. The type of worship found centered on Asherah was very much like the sexual worship connected with Ashtoreth.

How could the knowledge of the one true God survive if mankind was given to the polytheistic worship of many gods? Especially when worship had diminished to the extent that it appealed to man's depraved base instincts? God decided that He must enter into a relationship with a nation which would preserve the knowledge of monotheism—that there is only one God. Nations need not begin with large numbers. God chose one man to begin His covenant nation.

Abraham, Israel's Righteous Seed

Abram knew a great deal about polytheism. His father was an idol maker. He probably learned about the distinctions of the different family gods as a very young man. Surely his father would want him to carry on the family business. But God had other plans.

The Lord had said to Abram, "Leave your country, your people, and your father's household and go to the land I will show you. I will make you into a great nation and I will bless you; I will make your name great and you will be a blessing. I will bless those who bless you, and whoever curses you, I will curse; and all peoples on earth will be blessed through you." So Abram left as the Lord had told him; and Lot went with him. Abram was seventy-five years old when he set out from Haran.

Genesis 12:1-4

It is very important to move when God says "move" and to settle only when God says "settle." But it seems as if God was always too far for man to hear Him. In reality, God didn't move far away from man. Man moved away from God. God looked around the earth and He saw a man who was the kind of man who would raise up a family faithfully unto God. The God of generations, whose intention it was to build out of the loins of one man a great nation, made another master stroke.

God commanded Abram to leave everything that was familiar—his family, friends and livelihood—so that he could be formed into a great nation. It would be a nation that would preserve the knowledge of God and bless all the other peoples of the earth.

He said to Abram, "You are not only going to become the father of a nation, but through this nation, all other nations on the face of the earth are going to be blessed." God was not after Abram as a person. He only wanted a servant or an instrument. He was after the nations of the world.

Abram was faithful to God's call. He believed that God would give him a son. God gave Abram the covenant of circumcision as a sign that he and his descendants belonged to the Lord God. It was to be a distinctive covenant mark which would separate the males of this chosen nation from those of other nations.

> *Abram fell facedown and God said to him, "As for Me, this is My covenant with you: You will be the father of many nations. No longer will you be called Abram; your name will be Abraham, for I have made you a father of many nations..." Then God said to Abraham, "As for you, you must keep My covenant, you and your descendants after you for the generations to come. This is My covenant with you and your descendants after you, the covenant you are to keep: Every male among you shall be circumcised."*

> Genesis 17:3-5,9,10

Later, Abraham's son Isaac was given a renewal of the same promises given to him. Abraham's grandson, Jacob, had the covenant reconfirmed to him. He had twelve sons. Each of these sons had many children and developed into twelve tribes.

In the course of time, as generations progressed, this family became a large people. They went off into Egypt where God had prepared food for them during a time of famine. However, a later pharaoh of Egypt became harsh and tyrannical and made them his indentured servants. They were slaves for over four hundred years.

God remembered His covenant when they cried out to Him and asked for freedom from slavery. He heard their cries. God saw them in their distress and chose another man with a special destiny. He had hand-picked Moses to deliver the nation of Israel from the slavery of Egypt.

Moses, Israel's Deliverer

Moses was born in Egypt to parents who were slaves. That seems like a poor start in life, but he had another strike against him. Pharaoh had become jealous of the Jews and was afraid that they would grow into a strong nation. Therefore, he declared that every male child born in a Jewish family had to be killed at birth. The midwives who delivered Moses disobeyed the command of the king. Moses' mother was afraid that she would be caught breaking the law by raising a son, so she tried to hide him.

> *But when she could hide him no longer, she got a papyrus basket for him and coated it with tar and pitch. Then she placed the child in it and put it along the reeds along the bank of the Nile. His sister stood at a distance to see what would happen to him. Then Pharaoh's daughter went down to the Nile to bathe and her attendants were watching along the river bank. She saw the basket among the reeds and sent her slave girl to get it. She opened it and saw the baby. He was crying and she felt sorry for him. "This is one of the Hebrew babies," she said.*
>
> Exodus 2:3-6

God had selected Moses for a particular purpose. He was born a slave, but was raised by Pharaoh's daughter as heir to the throne of Egypt. He was allowed, while very young, to be cared for by his own parents since Pharaoh's daughter needed someone to nurse the child. Moses, however, rejected life in the court of the king and cleaved to the one true God he had learned about while living with his mother. God had selected a national deliverer.

But Moses intervened in a dispute. In defending his own fellow Israelite, he killed an Egyptian. Therefore, he became afraid. He needed to be schooled by God. He ran to the wilderness of Midian. There he helped raise the flocks of a priest named Jethro and married Jethro's daughter. While tending the flocks one day, he came near to the mountain of God. There Moses saw an amazing sight. A bush was in flames, but not consumed by the flame. The angel of the Lord, probably a reference to an Old Testament appearance of Jesus, spoke to Moses from the burning bush and declared:

> ... "I am the God of your father, the God of Abraham, the God of Isaac and the God of Jacob." At this Moses hid his face because he was afraid to look at God. The Lord said, "I have indeed seen the misery of my people in Egypt. I have heard them crying out because of their slave drivers, and I am concerned about their suffering. So I have come down to rescue them from the land of the Egyptians and to bring them up out of that land into a good and spacious land, a land flowing with milk and honey."
>
> Exodus 3:6-8

Moses immediately began to protest God's call to lead the Israelites out of Egypt. He made five protests to

God before God became angry with him. However, God allowed Moses to work with his brother Aaron when speaking with the people and Pharaoh.

God knew what Moses was to do before Moses had even been conceived. He had worked the circumstances of his life in a way that would prepare him to be a great leader of the people of God. Moses was a reluctant leader. He didn't see his own destiny. He had no idea of the kind of impact he would have on his nation Israel. Now we see clearly that God used Moses to change the very course of history. The world would be a very different place were it not for Moses. He impacted his nation, his world and the future.

The Israelites were miraculously delivered from slavery in Egypt. God brought judgment to the Egyptians and their false gods. The ten plagues on the Egyptians were all connected to false deities worshiped there. The Lord God proved that He was true and more powerful than any demons disguised as gods. Remember the destiny of Israel: God was preserving knowledge of Himself and preparing the way for all the nations of the world to be blessed.

Israel in the Wilderness

The Glory Cloud

God revealed Himself in a special way to the Israelites when He led them through the wilderness between Egypt and Canaan. They didn't understand His presence so God allowed them to catch a glimpse of His glory to stir their faith and remind them of who He is. From the time that God led the people out of Egypt, the Bible tells us He led them with a cloud that went before them in the daytime and a pillar of fire when it was dark. When they crossed the Red Sea, they saw the cloud of God's glory leading them.

In Exodus chapter sixteen, when they were encamping in the wilderness, the glory of God appeared before them so that they could rest under the cloud. When Moses went up into the mountain and the presence of the glory came down, what the people saw was a thick cloud of God's glory and of God's presence. God was separating a people unto Himself with these wonderful and miraculous signs of His presence.

The Mountain of God's Presence

In the third month after the Israelites left Egypt—on the very day—they came to the Desert of Sinai. After they had set out from Rephidim they entered the Desert of Sinai, and Israel camped there in the desert in front of the mountain.

Exodus 19:1-2

They didn't know it yet, but they were destined to stay there for some time. They went only to camp, but they stayed for forty years at the foot of a mountain. Now, mountains are very important. This mountain was to be very significant. It was already significant because Moses met God there. Where was God before? In Heaven. Where did Moses meet God? In the mountain.

Then Moses went up to God, and the Lord called to him from the mountain and said, "This is what you are to

say to the house of Jacob and what you are to tell the
people of Israel: You yourselves have seen what I did to
Egypt, and how I carried you on eagles' wings and
brought you to Myself. Now if you obey Me fully, and
keep My covenant, then out of all nations you will be
My treasured possession. Although the whole earth is
Mine, you will be for Me a kingdom of priests and a
holy nation. These are the words you are to speak to the
Israelites."

Exodus 19:3-6

Moses went up to God in the mountain. The Lord
called to him from that mountain and told him what to
say to the people he had led from Egypt. All along God
was looking down from Heaven and speaking to the
people from out of Heaven, but here we find God
making His sanctuary in the mountain and speaking
forth from out of the sanctuary to Moses. It was out of
the sanctuary of Heaven that He spoke to Noah and to
Abram. Out of the sanctuary of the mountain He gave
direction to Moses.

God said to Moses that day, "You yourselves have
seen what I did to Egypt and how I carried you on eagles'
wings, and how I brought you to myself." You can't get
to the Promised Land except you first meet the Lord of
the land. They must have been very excited because they
heard about this One who took them out of Egypt and
carried them on the wings of miracles to have an appointment with God. Where is this appointment?

The appointment was not simply of a place and time.
They were *appointed to obedience*. "Now if you obey Me

fully and keep My covenant, then out of all nations you will be My treasured possession. Although the whole earth is Mine, you will be for Me a kingdom of priests and a holy nation." These are the words Moses was commanded to share with the Israelites.

Out of the mountain God spoke to Moses and He told him to tell the people that they have a divine appointment, a responsibility to the One who had set them free from slavery. God wants, more than anything else, to come down and meet with His people because He is after the nations. From out of all the nations He chose a people and He separated them from other nations. He put them in the desert. He had an appointment with them at the mountain. He challenged them through Moses to fully obey Him.

Associated with the call to obedience was the promise of being God's unique, precious and chosen possession. The nation of Israel was to become a treasured possession, a holy nation and a kingdom of priests unto God. What a great honor and joy to have such direct and special access to the Almighty Creator of the universe.

Unfortunately, history has shown that the Israelites missed the most tremendous opportunity they could ever have had. That day Moses came down from the mountain and gave them the challenge, "The people all responded together, 'We will do everything the Lord has said' " (Exodus 19:8). They never kept this pledge. They were disobedient and unfaithful. That's why they stayed in the desert for forty years. However, God still had a plan for the nation. They never enjoyed all His blessing and privilege, but He used Israel in a tremendous way.

Moses went back to God and told Him how the people were pledged to obey. They promised to keep the covenant. But God knew some things that the people didn't. He is an awesome God.

And the Lord said to Moses, "Go to the people and con-secrate them today and tomorrow. Have them wash their clothes and be ready by the third day, because on that day the Lord will come down on Mount Sinai in the sight of all the people. Put limits for the people around the mountain and tell them, Be careful that you do not go up the mountain or touch the foot of it. Whoever touches the mountain shall surely be put to death."

Exodus 19:10-12

God wanted the people to consecrate themselves on the first day, dealing with those things within a man like attitudes, values or thought life. On the second day they were to wash their clothes and deal with their outer lives, their relationships, the external life. On the third day, they were destined to see Almighty God. God had an ap-pointment with His people.

The people agreed and they consecrated themselves the first day and washed their clothes on the second day. The morning of the third day, they probably were wait-ing with tremendous anticipation to meet this God who was so good to them.

When you're anticipating something like this, you don't want anything to interfere. You don't want bad weather. You don't want any unforeseen circumstance. There can be no distraction to an appointment like meeting God. Early the next morning, when they arose early in order to keep the appointment, the weather refused to cooperate. The Bible says that a thick cloud came down and lightning began to flash. The thunder rolled and the people became afraid. They may have thought that God would not come in all of this storm. This was too much turbulence.

God had already told Moses to tell them to come near when they heard the sound of trumpets blowing. When the trumpet began to sound from out of the heavens and billow through the mountain, God was calling forth His people and Moses summoned those weak, trembling-kneed people.

Then Moses led the people out of the camp to meet with God, and they stood at the foot of the mountain. Mount Sinai was covered with smoke, because the Lord descended on it with fire. The smoke billowed up from it like smoke from a furnace, the whole mountain trembled violently, and the sound of the trumpet grew louder and louder.

Exodus 19:17-19

They went to the foot of the mountain. They had been warned not to tread upon the presence of God's sanctuary. God had told Moses to put up limits and rails. He told him to post a guard so that the people would not, out of their exuberance, trespass on the holiness of God. There was little fear of them trespassing because they were already afraid from the dramatic display of nature before them. The Bible gives an awesome, pictureque and vivid description of this encounter between God and a nation.

I picture it like a massive volcanic flame that has just erupted from out of the belly of that big mountain. The entire mountain shook violently. God, the God of Heaven, Creator of the universe, only came down to the top of the mountain. The mountain couldn't handle it. The voice of the faithful God was heard and the people were afraid.

> *The Lord descended to the top of Mount Sinai and called Moses to the top of the mountain. So Moses went up...The Lord replied, "Go down and bring Aaron up with you. But the priests and the people must not force their way through to come up to the Lord, or He will break out against them."*
>
> Exodus 19:20,24

Israel and the Law

The day God visited the Israelites at the top of Mount Sinai was a day of destiny. It would forever be remembered by the descendants of Israel, but it would impact the remainder of the world as well. God proceeded to reveal His holiness to Moses and Aaron through the commands of the law. The Ten Commandments were the foundation, but they were only the beginning. God wanted the Israelites to be conformed to the lifestyle He wanted them to live. Justice, honesty, sexual propriety, ownership of property and all the various civil laws needed for a nation to be civilized, were given to Moses for the Israelites. These ten demands of God's covenant became the foundation of religion and law for Israel. The vast majority of legal and religious systems today are based on those same Ten Commandments.

Jews, Christians and the followers of Islam have revered the words of God on Mount Sinai as the foundation for life's activities ever since. England's common law and the constitutional governments that have developed since were based on the way God expected His people to treat one another as He presented the Ten Commandments to Moses and Aaron on Sinai.

When the people saw the thunder and lightening and heard the trumpet, and saw the mountain in smoke, they trembled with fear. They stayed at a distance and they said to Moses, "Speak to us yourself and we will listen, but do not have God speak to us, or we will die." Moses said to the people, "Do not be afraid. God has come to test you, so that the fear of God will be with you to keep you from sinning."

Exodus 20:18-20

The children of Israel were pleading for direction. "Where do we go from here?" Having camped in the desert, already grumbling and dissatisfied, they were crying out for an answer. Yet they were afraid of the awesomeness of God. When the voice of direction came, the people stood at a distance and said: "Speak to us yourself and we will listen. But do not have God speak to us or we will die" (Exodus 20:19). Moses explained to the people that God had come to test them and to try them so the fear of God could keep them from sinning. The people still remained at a distance while Moses approached the thick darkness where God was.

Did Israel become God's treasured possesion? Did they become a holy nation? Was the law sufficient to make them God's kingdom of priests among the nations of the world? The nation of Israel as a whole never really fulfilled its destiny. However, God's purpose was not deterred. He chose, from among the people, a tribe to preserve His purpose. The prophetic purpose of this tribe is the subject of the next chapter.

Chapter Four

God's Sanctuary in the Nation (Old Testament)

The law of God was not designed to elicit blind obedience to rules. What God wanted was a relationship with His people. The law exposed their unrighteousness and revealed the gap between a sinful people and a holy God. He wanted them to be increasingly more mature and more like Him in His holiness. He wanted to be with them, yet they could not accept His presence in all His glory. God did not intend for this nation of people to grow to be a blessing without His presence.

While they were in the wilderness, Moses was spending time with God. He spent forty days and forty nights on the mountain. He went up the mountain with God two or three times. However, the people were down there in the wilderness obeying their own counsel. Following their own best thoughts and being captured by their own desires, they returned to a world of pagan darkness, a world of immorality and perversion. While Moses was at the top of the mountain, they polluted themselves by returning to the heathen worship of an idol.

God was expressly disappointed that they couldn't trust Him for even a few days. Moses interceded in prayer and God spared the nation from annihilation.

How could God make this nation a blessing to other nations when they couldn't even keep an appointment with Him because they were afraid of His presence? They couldn't be faithful for more than a few days. Must God remain in the heavens and direct the affairs of the world? Can God remain localized in a mountain? How can He become the kind of personal God He wants to be when mankind is so very unlike Him?

The Tabernacle in the Wilderness

God had a plan! He established a portable tabernacle, a localized sanctuary, where the people could identify His presence and worship Him.

The Lord said to Moses, "Tell the Israelites to bring Me an offering. You are to receive the offering for Me from each man whose heart prompts him to give. These are the offerings you are to receive from them: gold, silver, and bronze; blue, purple and scarlet yarn and fine linen; goat hair; ram skins dyed red and hides of sea cows; acacia wood; olive oil for the light; spices for the anointing oil and for the fragrant incense; and onyx stones and other gems to be mounted on the ephod and breast piece."

Exodus 25:1-7

God spoke to Moses and told him to tell the people to bring their offerings, their precious metals and jewels. They were to contribute their resources to fulfill God's plan. In the next few verses it reads:

Then have them make a sanctuary for Me and I will dwell among them. Make this tabernacle and all of its furnishings exactly like the pattern I will show you.

Exodus 25:8-9

God gave specific instructions: "Take all of their precious belongings and have them make for Me a sanctuary so that I may dwell among them." By dwelling in that sacred place, He would be among the people. Moses followed the prescribed instructions of God. He made for God a tabernacle, sometimes called the tent of meeting. It was the place of appointment, the sanctuary of the living God.

The God of the sanctuary of Heaven who came down to the sanctuary of the great mountain now had come down into the sanctuary of the tabernacle of meeting, which was structured according to the spiritual tabernacle in the heavens.

There was an outer court and the Holy Place, along with the Most Holy Place where the Ark of the Covenant was. The tabernacle is not a tabernacle without the Ark. The presence of God would come down over the Most

Holy Place as a cloud to guide the people. So God had them then prepare a sanctuary or a place of meeting.

The Call of the Firstborn

God's next objective was to call out from among them a priestly family. They would become His kingdom of priests: a remnant of people who communed with God. In order to make them a priestly community, He decided to claim them as His firstborn. The culture of that day better understood than we do in our time that the firstborn is very precious.

The firstborn was the first one to come forth. There was tremendous joy and satisfaction. There was a sense of fulfillment just to know that you could have offspring. The firstborn was given the inheritance of his father in those days. In time, the Jews actually passed a law that prescribed a procedure where two-thirds of the inheritance went to the firstborn, and the other third went to the rest of the children. That doesn't sound fair, does it? Wouldn't you have liked to have been the firstborn?

Actually, the firstborn was given that inheritance because it was accompanied by personal responsibility. The responsibility of the firstborn was to insure the perpetuity of the name of his father. The firstborn was challenged to enhance, by his own fruitfulness and productivity, the possessions of his father's estate. The firstborn was responsible to look after the widow, his mother, when his father died. He also had to insure that the entire household of brothers and sisters were properly cared for. It would have been a shame, which carried a social stigma, for any member of the family to lack any good thing. The firstborn had a tremendous responsibility indeed.

The firstborn received from the estate the provisions adequate to manage or to meet his responsibility. This helps us understand the story of Esau trading his birthright for a bowl of beans. Imagine giving up your entire inheritance for a bowl of beans! He was not being generous to his brother Jacob, however. What he really did was abdicate his responsibility. It was Jacob who carried on the line of his father. Jacob was renamed Israel, which means overcomer. Thus the heritage of the entire nations is attributed to the younger brother rather than the firstborn, who forfeited the honor.

To whomever you give the firstborn, or the firstfruit, you know that person is "el numero uno," that is, "number one!" When I pick the first mango from the tree, what do I do with it? I eat it myself. I place myself first, making my position come before all the others. If I take it to the pastor and his wife, it is like giving it unto God, giving thanks and recognizimg Him as my source. It is a celebration of my faith in God. Above all, when I give away the firstfruit, I know that a harvest is to follow. God sees to it.

Remember what God did in Egypt? He destroyed the firstborn of Egypt. All the inheritance was deposited in the heir to the throne. All the time, education, resources and hopes that were placed in the firstborn children of Egypt were dashed when God wiped out the firstborn.

However, He preserved the Israelites and never allowed the death angel to kill their firstborn. When they came across the Red Sea, God expected a commitment in response to His loving provision for their children. He said to the Israelites, "You're Mine, and therefore I am claiming your firstborn."

The nation did not become a people of God until they were willing to place Him first by giving God their firstborn. When you see how Israel became a grumbling, resistant and rebellious people, from the time they went across the Red Sea, you realize that God was not pleased with them. I believe they were not willing to commit their firstborn to God. Their problems came from the fact that they were not giving God first place in their lives. They were seeking their own selfish interests rather than God's interests.

The Call of the Levites

God had a plan. He is after the nations. Notice what He did.

*After you have purified the Levites and presented them as a wave offering, they are to come to do their work at the Tent of Meeting. They are the Israelites who are to be given wholly to Me. I have taken them as My own in place of the firstborn, the first male offspring from every Israelite woman. Every firstborn male in Israel, whether man or animal, is Mine. When I struck down all the firstborn in Egypt, I set them apart for Myself. **And I have taken the Levites in place of all the firstborn sons in Israel.** Of all the Israelites, I have given the*

Levites as gifts to Aaron and his sons to do the work at the Tent of Meeting on behalf of the Israelites and to make atonement for them so that no plague will strike the Israelites when they go near the sanctuary.

Numbers 8:15-19

What was this sanctuary? It was the Tent of Meeting, where God would come down so He might be among them. God not only separated a place for Himself, but He also chose a people, a tribe, to serve Him and thus preserve the whole nation. The tribe had no possessions given to them from out of the world, but their possessions were provided from everything that was given unto God by the people. God's resources became theirs as they ministered unto God and as they would make atonement on behalf of the nation. As they would protect their nation from the plagues and from the wrath of God in the sanctuary, they were blessed to eat the offerings and sacrifices made there by the people.

The Tent of Meeting was placed outside of the camp. All the tents from all of the tribes were set at a distance. Around the Tent of Meeting were the tents of the Levitical tribe, which was there to guard the presence of God, or to protect the people from the presence of God. Therefore *they protected and preserved the nation from the wrath of God*. This was to become a primary function of God's chosen people in the midst of an ungodly nation.

You may recall that God promised Abraham He would make a nation from his descendants which would bless all the nations of the earth. When the whole world was filled with the paganistic worship of many gods, Israel stood alone proclaiming the truth of the one Almighty God. They proclaimed His holiness by preserving the expectations of the law. They communed with Him through a calendar full of festivals, feasts and sacrifices. When you read in the Books of Leviticus and Numbers, you discover that the Levitical tribe is the one that had the responsibility to serve God at the tabernacle. The priests were from a particular family. They were descendants of Aaron. However, Aaron was also from the tribe of Levi.

The responsibility of the Levites and the priests was to minister unto God. They were to ascribe greatness, honor and praise to Him. Physically, they tended to the structure, the actual setting of tabernacle and its furnishings. They kept the door, prepared all the holy articles and supported the priests. The Levites assisted in the sacrifices. They were also responsible for bearing the iniquity of the altar; that is, for bearing the sins of their people before God and making atonement on behalf of the nation. *In this way they were protecting the nation from the wrath of God.*

The priests and the Levites had to perform the sacrifices that would minister unto God and that would satisfy Him for the sins and the iniquity of the people. When they did that, they would go from the brazen altar outside the outer court to performing their duties within the inner court until they came to the altar of incense. They sprinkled blood on that altar. They gave praise and offered their prayers unto God. Once a year the high priest, and only he alone, would enter into the Most Holy Place and sprinkle the Ark of the Covenant with blood and with incense.

Then God would come down, God's glory would fill the Most Holy Place and the nation would know they were in right standing with God. They knew that God had heard them. They could then get the counsel of God. In the early days, Moses and Aaron heard from God whenever they went into the Tabernacle. God's presence had come and filled it.

Now Moses used to take a tent and pitch it outside the camp some distance away, calling it the "tent of meeting." Anyone inquiring of the Lord would go to the tent of meeting outside the camp...As Moses went into the tent, the pillar of cloud would come down and stay at the entrance, while the Lord spoke with Moses. Whenever the people saw the pillar of cloud standing at the entrance to the tent, they all stood and worshipped, each at the entrance to his tent.

Exodus 33:7,9-10

Whenever the people wanted direction, they would go toward the tent of meeting. They no longer would go to the mountain. They wouldn't cry out to the heavens, but go to the place of appointment. "Whenever Moses went out to the tent, all the people rose and stood at the entrance to their tents" (v. 8). In other words, the people did not go into the tabernacle; they dared not. They would look toward the tent, rise and watch Moses go into the tent.

As Moses went into the tent, the pillar of cloud would come down and stay at the entrance while the Lord spoke with Moses. Whenever the people saw the pillar of cloud standing at the entrance to the tent, they all stood and worshiped, each at the entrance to his tent. "The Lord would speak to Moses face to face, as a man speaks with his friend. Then Moses would return to the camp, but his young aide Joshua, son of Nun remained in the tent" (Exodus 33:11).

The sanctuary that God had Moses build became the place of instruction, counsel and direction. Whenever the people saw the cloud, they knew that the glory of God had come down. His presence had come to visit the nation and, in that way, God dwelt among them.

Israel and the Church

I would like to make an important distinction between Israel and the Church. Israel was a nation. Sometimes we like to equate the Church to Israel. But Paul is very careful to tell us that it's not all of natural Israel that is equated with the Church. Not all that is the seed of Abraham is the Church. It is only the seed which is after Christ. "In other words, it is not the natural children who are God's children, but it is the children of the promise who are regarded as Abraham's offspring" (Romans 9:8).

The Church maintains a distinct identity from that of the nation in the same way that the priestly tribe of Levi was separated from the other tribes of the nation of Israel. The nation never fulfilled their call as priests unto God. But God chose from out of the nation a people who would become priests unto Him on behalf of the nation. Hence it is more precise to identify the New Testament Church with the priestly tribe of Levi in the midst of the nation of Israel, than with Israel itself.

The priests of any generation are the firstfruit of their nation. If the firstfruit are holy, then the whole nation is sanctified unto God. If the people of God, as the firstfruit of the nation, offer themselves as a living sacrifice unto God, it insures that a rich harvest would follow. As Paul said, "If the part of the dough offered as firstfruits is holy, then the whole batch is holy; If the root is holy, so are the branches" (Romans 11:16).

Through the course of time, the tabernacle in the wilderness became the temple in the city. What the tabernacle was to a wandering, traveling people, whether in battle or as they camped, the temple became for a nation that was settled in the land of promise in Canaan. Whenever the nation disregarded the temple, it went through upheaval and devastation. If the nation is to be restored, first the temple must be restored.

It is interesting to note that God never used Israel to curse other nations but He did use other nations to judge Israel. After Solomon's temple was destroyed, the people went into captivity. God used the pagan empire of Babylon to chastise His people Israel. But then they returned with Nehemiah and Ezra and the temple of Zerubabbel was built. The establishment of a nation has no guarantee of the presence of the glory of God unless the temple is established. The temple was designed so that when God came into His sanctuary, He could dwell among them.

The story is told in the Book of Ezra that the glory of that temple was so awesome and tremendously overwhelming, that those who knew the glory of the former temple praised God. They shouted. They were overwhelmed. A cry went out so loud that no one could tell the difference between a shout, a cry or a praise. Men and women were beside themselves with tremendous joy and elation. For miles one could hear them praising the living God because the temple of God's presence was reestablished.

That temple still experienced problems during the course of its history. You need to remember that there were people like Hezekiah who, while restoring his nation, first restored the temple. He opened again the temple of the Lord. There were also those like Josiah, who rediscovered the Word and saw the purpose of the temple. He reestablished the temple worship in the midst of a very difficult time for the nation.

You cannot restore a nation and you cannot change a world, until the Church is first changed. It is from the Church that the instruction, the authority and the direction comes. It is from out of the temple of the living God in the place of the Ark of the Covenant, with the covenant law and instruction of God and the rod of authority of the priests, that revival and change develop.

When Moses instructed the people from out of the tabernacle, the glory of God so filled the tabernacle that the people saw the presence of the glory of God was there. The instructions of God came to Moses from out of the presence of the glory cloud of God Almighty.

The tragedy recorded in Ezekiel chapter ten is that when the nation became a reprobate people, the glory departed from the temple. This had been revealed to Ezekiel in a vision. However, God gave to this land a new vision. It was one in which God again revealed His desire to dwell amongst a nation people. There Ezekiel saw the restoration of his people. So you cannot have restoration of a world without restoration of the temple and God made ample plans for that, as reflected in Ezekiel's vision.

There must be a restoration of the presence and communion that comes from knowing God. God, sitting in the high heavens, in the heavenly tabernacle, had counsel with Himself and decided that He really wanted to come down from out of the throne of Heaven to visit His people in a new temple. How was this manifested reality of God to become more permanent, more of a permeating presence within the nation? If the people of God were to become the source of spiritual strength for the nation, what would be the vessel that could replace the tabernacle and the temple?

This manifested presence would have to come out of the very Being of God, become visible on the earth yet still contain the essence, divinity and nature of God! It would have to be a created body which would become the very dwelling place of God. He decided to make Himself a body! The Bible says, "A body you prepared for Me" (Heb. 10:5).

In the Old Testament it is very clear that God established Israel with a purpose:

The Lord said to Abram, "Leave your country and your people and your father's household and go to the land I will show you. I will make you into a great nation and I will bless you; I will make your name great and you will be a blessing. I will bless those who bless you and whoever curses you I will curse; and all peoples on earth will be blessed through you."

Genesis 12:1-3

Through Abram and his seed, all other nations would be blessed—not cursed, not destroyed, but blessed. Through Israel the gift of the Messiah, Immanuel—God with us—would be given and the message of the gospel taken to all nations. No other nation on the face of the earth can claim that same purpose for existing. The Israelites preserved knowledge of God for all the nations. They prepared the way for the Messiah, Jesus Christ, to give us a new temple, one not made by human hands. It is this Body of Christ that is challenged to uphold the purpose for the nations today.

Chapter Five

God's Sanctuary Among the Nations (New Testament)

In the Old Testament, God used Israel as an example people to speak to the nations of the world. God is using, in New Testament times, His people, the Church, to be a blessing to the nations.

> *Then Jesus came to them and said, "All authority in heaven and on earth has been given to Me. Therefore go and make disciples of all nations, baptizing them in the name of the Father and of the Son and of the Holy Spirit, and teaching them to obey everything I have commanded you. And surely I am with you always, to the very end of the age."*
>
> Matthew 28:17-20

The Church has missed the full dimension of this great commission when it only tries to make disciples of individuals. What about the nations? To make the nations into disciples is to turn the nations to following the principles of the Word of God. It is the challenge to let the laws, culture and moral values of a nation be determined by the unsearchable, eternal and final Word from God. This Word is found in the Holy Bible, the Scriptures.

In order to understand this idea of the nature and concept of the Church, we must look at the founder of the Church, Jesus. He was so much more than merely a man. In John chapter one it is recorded, "In the beginning was the Word, and the Word was with God, and the Word was God, He was with God in the beginning." (v. 1). The passage goes on to say that He came down and He tabernacled, or lived for awhile, among men.

Jesus: The Tabernacle of God

A tabernacle is a tent or temporary dwelling. Christ lived in a human body for a temporary period of time. This was not His permanent state. He became a man and took on human form. The tabernacle was called "Jesus." He was the sanctuary of God, Immanuel, God with us.

For thirty-three years that Tabernacle was carried through the dusty streets of Galilee and Samaria and into Jerusalem. That Tabernacle that knew no sin judged the Old Testament temple and religious system. He cleansed it and He said, "Destroy this Temple, and I will raise it up again in three days" (John 2:19). They thought He was talking about the temple built by hands. They did not know He was talking about the Temple that was specially fashioned and formed in the womb of Mary. That Temple was the implanted seed by the Holy Ghost.

Jesus: the Sacrifice and the Priest of God

That Temple was to become not only a Temple, but also the very sacrifice to be brought to the altar of Almighty God. He was the Place of Meeting. He was the Sacrifice to be offered, and He Himself became the one to do it, so He also became the priest. Why could He do it Himself? The Bible tells us that He was God's only begotten Son. "He is the image of the invisible God, **the firstborn** over all creation" (Colossians 1:15).

As the firstborn, all authority belonged to Him. As the high priest, He took the lamb and placed it on the brazen altar outside the sanctuary. It wasn't for the benefit of the high priest, it was for a world that His Father loved. Christ gave up His body as a Lamb slain for our sins. He Himself had no sin. If He had wanted to preserve the Tabernacle of His body, then He would not have gone to the cross. The truth is that God was not after the Body, He was after the nations. The sacrifice of Himself made atonement so that the nations could be reconciled to the Father.

You may recall how God called Israel as His covenant nation in order to preserve the truth of the one Almighty God who created the world and in order for it to be a blessing to all nations. Israel met this purpose in that Christ came from Israel and gave Himself as a sacrifice for all of mankind.

Moses instituted a system of sacrifices among the Levites and priests. They included the Burnt Offering, where the animal was completely consumed by flames.

This signified the total devotion of the people to God. Another sacrifice was the Meal Offering, which was a gift of breads and cakes to show fellowship with God. The Peace Offering was designed to reconcile man with God, or to bring justification. The Sin Offering paid the penalty for man's sins. The Guilt Offering reconciled man to God as his guilt was paid for by the sacrifice. The Guilt Offering was usually made for sins committed unintentionally. There were also Wave Offerings and Drink Offerings, which expressed gratitude for God's provision.

All of these sacrifices were made by the Israelites as a way of looking forward by faith to the work of Jesus. Christ Jesus gave Himself as a complete and total sacrifice. He was all of those sacrifices combined in one perfect sacrifice for all time.

Jesus: Triumphing Over Sin and the Grave

After the sacrifice of Christ, His body was placed in a brand new tomb. In the spirit He went down and took the keys of death and of Hades from satan. He led away captives that were there, Abraham, Moses, Isaiah and other saints from long ago. They held their tokens there waiting, to cash them in, so they could make it to Heaven. The Bible tells us that some of these saints were seen walking through Jerusalem looking over the old city during that weekend (Matthew 27:52-53).

My inspired imagination tells me that Christ came back to the tomb and picked up His body. Once again all nature responded to its Creator. "There was a violent earthquake, for an angel of the Lord came down from heaven and, going to the tomb, rolled back the stone and sat on it" (Matthew 28:2). His body was transformed so that mortality put on immortality. He was able to take back His life because when He took the keys from satan, He took the authority over death, hell and the grave. That body had known no sin of its own, so death and hell had no legal claim to it.

It was Sunday morning when He revealed His resurrection to His disciples. "Sunday mornings" are very important, you understand. We all go through problems sometimes. Like a proverbial Friday night, we feel like we have been nailed to a cross. You have to tell the devil, "Sunday's coming." There is no problem in this life that will stop resurrection Sunday from coming.

For forty days Christ walked around with His resurrected body. He met with some of His close associates. Some had run away. Others had denied Him. But He gathered them together. The resurrection gave them proof of His identity as the true Messiah.

Earlier, Jesus had attempted to comfort them by saying:

Do not let your hearts be troubled. Trust in God, trust also in Me. In My Father's house are many rooms; if it were not so, I would have told you. I am going there to prepare a place for you. And if I go and prepare a place for you, I will come back and take you to be with Me that you also may be where I am.

John 14:1-3

Jesus had come back from death. "...are you at this time going to restore the kingdom to Israel?" they asked

(Acts 1:6). They were looking for a temporal kingdom here on earth. One had already said that he wanted to sit on the right side of the king. Another thought he might deserve the left. I would imagine that they thought things were really going to be all right now. Instead Jesus gave them the commission to disciple the nations and said, "Do not leave Jerusalem, but wait for the gift My Father promised, which you have heard Me speak about. For John baptized with water, but in a few days you will be baptized with the Holy Spirit" (Acts 4b-5). They would know the direction to go once they received the Holy Spirit.

> *After the Lord Jesus had spoken to them, He was taken up into heaven and He sat at the right hand of God. Then the disciples went out and preached everywhere, and the Lord worked with them and confirmed His word by the signs that accompanied it.*
>
> Mark 16:19-20

It was while He was deliberating with them that a cloud came. The cloud received Him into it. It was a natural cloud, but also a cloud of God's presence. The cloud speaks to us symbolically of Heaven. The cloud is part of the celestial or physical heavens. It also represents for us the presence of God. When you see the cloud, remember that the Israelites were guided by the cloud. Where the cloud rested, they stayed. The cloud gave direction. The cloud came and ushered Christ Jesus up to Heaven to be with His Father.

He left this earth, having condemned the temple that was built with hands. He wept over the city and said, "O

Jerusalem, Jerusalem, you who kill the prophets and stone those sent to you, how often have I longed to gather your children together, as a hen gathers her chicks under her wings, but you were not willing" (Luke 13:34). Referring to the temple, Jesus asked, "Do you see all these things?...I tell you the truth, not one stone here will be left on another..." (Matthew 24:2).

Paul tells us in the Book of Hebrews that Christ ascended into Heaven and entered into that more glorious tabernacle that is not made by man, nor is it part of this creation. It is a greater and more glorious tabernacle. He is seated at the right hand of His Father as our High Priest to hear all our confessions. However, what about the tabernacle among the nations?

The Church: God's Firstfruit

Jesus had said to His disciples, "Remain in Jerusalem," and they did. Sometimes I wonder whether they were obeying Him or were just too frightened to take to the streets. But they were together in prayer on the day of Pentecost, fifty days after Passover. Pentecost signifies the Feast of the Firstfruits (Leviticus 23:17). It is the festival that anticipates the harvest to come. The Jews also celebrated it for the giving of the Law of God.

I believe members of every nation were there, because the Bible says people came from every nation that was known. They had gathered in Jerusalem. Thousands of people were celebrating Firstfruits and the Law of God. God had something that He wanted to do for the nations that were represented there. The Bible tells us that, while the disciples were together in that upper room, God the Holy Spirit burst forth from out of Heaven. He came down as fire and rested upon the heads of the people of God. He caused them to speak in tongues and to proclaim the word of God boldly. Every nation and every individual could hear the word, the gospel of the Kingdom, proclaimed in their own language.

> *When the day of Pentecost came, they were all together in one place. Suddenly a sound like the blowing of a violent wind came from heaven and filled the whole house where they were sitting. They saw what seemed to be tongues of fire that separated and came to rest on each of them. All of them were filled with the Holy Spirit and began to speak in other tongues as the spirit enabled them.*
>
> Acts 2:1-4

I believe that on that day, Jesus was celebrated as the Firstfruit of them that shall be raised. Whenever the firstfruit is picked and offered unto God, it is sure that the harvest will follow. He who was first called the Only Begotten is now called the Firstborn, because there are many brothers born in the Kingdom because of His work. He is not ashamed to call us brothers (Hebrews 2:11).

He sees mankind captured as slaves in the marketplaces of the nations and has become the Redeemer-Kinsman receiving us as brothers. With His own blood He has purchased us. I imagine Him taking us into His house that He has prepared for us and presenting us to His Father for adoption. John 1:12 tells us, "Yet to all who received Him, to those who believed in His name, He gave the right to become the children of God." Paul tells us that, as adopted sons, we are also given His Spirit (Romans 8:15).

He accepts us the way we are. It's one thing to be legally adopted; it's another thing to have the very spirit and nature of the family into which you are adopted. You begin to grow from glory to glory and to look like the One who adopted you. We are both legal and spiritual brothers of the Firstborn.

All who trust in Christ are therefore heirs of God. And not simply heirs, but joint heirs with the Firstborn. All the wealth given to the eldest is shared with the younger sons. "For no matter how many promises God has made, they are 'Yes' in Christ" (2 Cor. 1:20a). "All authority in heaven and on earth has been given to me," said Jesus. "Therefore go and make disciples of all nations..." (Matthew 28:18b-19). Peter declares, "His divine power has given us everything we need for life and godliness..." (2 Pet. 1:3).

The Church: God's Temple

On the Day of Pentecost, the Body that was taken up into the sanctuary of Heaven poured out its Spirit to another body gathered in the upper room in Jerusalem. We have become the natural Body of Christ, connected to the supernatural Head which is at the right hand of the Father in Heaven. We are the temple of God among the nations!

The apostle Paul affirms in the epistle to the Colossians that Christ is the Head of the Body (Colossians 1:18). He is not on earth, but His Body is. That is why the vital unity between the Head and the Body is very important and should never be divorced. Paul calls the relationship between Christ and the Church a mystery.

There is no other body on the face of this earth that has both a natural Body and a divine Head. What the world can see is the natural Body. The Body must give them evidence that there is a Head. That Body started in the wilderness when God said to Moses, "build Me a sanctuary that I might dwell among them." The tabernacle in the wilderness became the temple in the city.

In New Testament times, God does not live in temples made by hands. Jesus Christ Himself said:

And I tell you that you are Peter, and on this rock I will build My church, and the gates of Hades will not overcome it. I will give you the keys to the kingdom of heaven; whatever you bind on earth will be bound in heaven, and whatever you loose on earth will be loosed in heaven.

Matthew 16:18-19

Again, I tell you that if two of you on earth agree about anything you ask for, it will be done for you by My Father in heaven. For where two or three come together in My name, there am I with them.

Matthew 18:19-20

The cloud of God's presence is the Spirit of the living God who has come to guide us into all truth. He will convict the world of sin, of righteousness and of judgment to come. He will also be the Comforter, the One who stands by us and undergirds us, and the One who counsels us and directs us according to the instruction of the Word of God.

I'm referring here to the temple made from living stones, which temple is the house of God. I am talking about not only a place, but also a people who are firstborn, not in the natural, but having been born again from above after the order of the priesthood of Christ. **From out of every nation, every kindred, every language, every people, He has purchased for Himself a kingdom of priests unto Him so that they may rule in the earth.**

A world that is lost needs to hear from a people who are found. A world without direction will listen to people who have found their purpose. It is for this reason that the first step for us as the Church is not to be an army, but a sanctuary. The direction that the world needs can only come from out of the counsel of the Ark of the Most Holy Place. And the people who give that direction can only be priests who themselves live within the presence of the sanctuary in holiness and righteousness unto God.

Therefore, God is looking for a people who are prepared to be priests before they are kings; priests before they are prophets. He is looking for a kingdom of intercessors. That's an awesome task. Through them, He can dwell among the nations and in the world.

This message is to be received by priests in the sanctuary. It must be filtered through the center of the

Most Holy Place. Any time we go out into the camp, we must go out from under the cloud or be led by the cloud. Otherwise we'll be like those who grumbled and rebelled in the wilderness because they were caught up and led by their own desires and their own humanistic views.

The holy nation became the Church of Jesus Christ, a holy people and royal priesthood, a holy nation of people belonging to God. From old Israel to the New Covenant people—the Church—we are a nation among the nations. We must understand that God has set a plan in place to make the whole earth come under His rulership and that this is to be expected through His people.

> *But you are a chosen people, a royal priesthood, a holy nation, a people belonging to God, that you may declare the praises of Him who called you out of darkness into His wonderful light. Once you were not a people, but now you are the people of God; once you had not received mercy, but now you have received mercy.*
>
> 1 Peter 1:9-10

The tabernacle in the wilderness became the temple in the city. Now the temple in the city has become the Body of Christ among the peoples of the world. God is in control. He established the nations. He chose Israel to preserve the knowledge of God and pave the way for the Christ to come. Today the Church sits in the midst of the nation as God's sanctuary.

The whole created world groans, travails and waits for the manifestation of the sons of God (Romans 8:19-22). God wants to reconcile all things to Himself. He will use nations for His purposes, and He will use the holy nation, which is His Church, to bring all things back to Himself. Join me now as we find out more particularly God's purpose in establishing the nations.

Chapter Six

The Purpose of the Nations

God has structured nations and determined the exact places where each nation will have its jurisdiction. The times when each nation will be established and overturned are determined by the sovereign will of God. But, "Blessed is the nation whose God is the Lord" (Psalm 33:12).

I'm challenged by the dramatic picture of Psalm 2. It begins, "Why do the nations conspire and the peoples plot in vain?" (Psalm 2:1).

Autonomous man proudly leads nations and propagates ungodly philosophies in his attempts to build political systems independent of God. The inevitable result is his own destruction.

It doesn't matter what the authorities are doing. The Psalmist says heathens rage. People imagine vain things. Kings of the earth take counsel together, against the

Lord and against His anointed. History will prove that He who sits in the heavens laughs at the efforts of the rebellious men of the world. He laughs at the parliamentary deliberations which are contrary to His will. He will hold them in derision. Then He will rebuke them in His anger and terrify them in His wrath. The Bible says, "Yet I have installed My king on Zion, My holy hill" (Psalm 2:6). "When the righteous thrive [rule], the people rejoice; when the wicked rule the people groan" (Proverbs 29:2).

Ultimately, God will cause the nations to accomplish His will. Let us examine why He chose to organize the world into nations.

Redeeming the Land

Nations are established by God for two purposes. First, it is God's plan and purpose that the whole earth be inhabited by men. "From one man He made every nation of men that they should inhabit the whole earth; and He determined the times set for them and the exact places where they should live" (Acts 17:26). Compare also Isaiah 45:8 and 9.

"To inhabit the whole earth" means more than simply occupying space. It means making the land habitable. God gave mankind dominion over the earth. Although the command has been misapplied and abused many times since the fall, it is still God's directive to mankind.

What is man that You are mindful of him, the son of man that You care for him? You made him a little lower than the heavenly beings and crowned him with glory

74

and honor. You made him ruler over the works of Your hands; You put everything under his feet.

Psalm 8:4-6

Mankind is divided into nations to cultivate the land. Therefore God expects good management of all the resources found on the earth because they belong to God. Mankind is a steward, or manager, of God's wealth in the earth.

Man must also organize for his survival. Nations are the means whereby we must cooperate to provide basic utilities, produce adequate crops, restrain lawless citizens and provide adequate protection against external oppressors. All of these things are included in making the land habitable.

Inhabiting the land is a responsibility entrusted to us by God. When a child has no parents and is unable to make decisions for himself, a trustee may be appointed to watch over the interests and affairs of the child until he reaches maturity. Similarly, God is allowing the nations to watch over His resources in trust, until the Church is ready to claim its full inheritance. This divine intention of God is declared throughout the Scriptures. "His descendants (i.e., the man that fears the Lord) will inherit the land" (See Psalm 25:12-13).

At present, heathen nations appear to have dominance on the earth. Christians remain on the sidelines, as disinterested victims. Many see themselves as squatters on the land nervously enduring with grim determination until the Lord returns to rescue them from the threat of the enemy. I have discovered the exciting truth that nations will rise and fall under the sovereign rule of God until the fullness of time when the meek will inherit the earth (Matthew 5:5).

> *For evil men will be cut off, but those who hope in the Lord will inherit the land. A little while and the wicked will be no more; though you look for them they will not be found. But the meek will inherit the land and enjoy great peace.*
>
> Psalm 37:9-11

Indeed, the whole creation groans and travails, waiting in eager expectation for the sons of God to be revealed. "In hope that the creation itself will be liberated from its bondage to decay and brought into the glorious freedom of the children of God" (Romans 8:21). "In that day the kingdoms of this world will become the Kingdom of our Lord and of His Christ and He will reign for ever and ever" (Revelation 11:15). Until then we can only reign with Him to the extent we exercise the potential God has given to us to triumph over the enemy in the earth.

Redeeming the People

The second reason God organized the world into nations is so men could find Him. "God did this so that men would seek Him and perhaps reach out for Him and find Him though He is not far from any one of us" (Acts 17:27).

God established nations to be a type of marketplace from which Jesus Christ would purchase men to become another nation, a kingdom of priests. As a kingdom of priests, they will rule on the earth. Revelation chapter five tells us of a new song sung in Heaven.

And they sang a new song, "You are worthy to take the scroll and to open its seals, because You were slain, and with Your blood You purchased men for God from every tribe and language and people and nation. You have made them to be a kingdom and priests to serve our God, and they will reign on the earth."

Revelation 5:9-10

Nations provide the context within which men may find God. It was extremely difficult to find God in the wild, prehistoric times. The task is as challenging in the wild rat race of our "modern civilization." God has to domesticate us within prescribed local communities to communicate with us.

He may bring a missionary into a land to reach the lost souls living there. Perhaps He brings an evangelist to speak with thousands at one time. God has placed a common thread within the civilized cultures of the world so that mankind will believe the message. "This is good and pleases God our Savior who wants all men to be saved and come to a knowledge of the truth" (1 Timothy 2:4).

The nations have a responsibility to structure themselves into harvest fields for establishing and expanding the Kingdom of God. God expects national leaders to be responsive to Him and to the message. Nineveh repented and was spared. The leadership of that ancient pagan nation believed God's warning through Jonah, and encouraged the people to repent. How much more should our civilized democracies help pave the way for the gospel seed to flourish in the hearts of the citizens.

> *I urge then, first of all, that requests, prayers, intercession and thanksgiving be made for everyone—for kings and all those in authority that we may live peaceful and quiet lives in all godliness and holiness.*
>
> 1 Timothy 2:1-3

God wants human beings to be saved. It pleases Him that people come to a knowledge of the truth. He has placed a responsibility on the nations that they must provide a culture, setting and environment that facilitates the gospel message.

Good Government

No nation can fulfill its purpose without due consideration to good government. Government means to direct, control, restrain and influence a people within a given environment. Government manages all its available resources for the good of the people and to the glory of God's will. Hence Paul commands us to be thankful for the rulers, kings and authorities over us. He also commands intercessory prayer on behalf of our governmental leaders.

A further word on government is necesary. There are different spheres and types of government in operation today. Usually when one thinks of government, the capital city of our nation comes to mind. Government is most often equated with civil authorities and central rulership.

Running for government is usually equated with getting involved in civil politics. When I was a teenager, there was a course in school called "Civics." Today, the same course is called "Government." This change in the meaning and use of the word "government" has significantly affected the structure and rule of society.

Interestingly, the dictionary definition of the word "government" reflects this change over the years. The 1828 edition of Webster's Dictionary of the English language defines government as direction and regulation. This edition went on to explain that the direction and regulation of the government controlled our conduct. It commented that men are apt to neglect government because of our temper and passions. Obviously, the definition of government in 1828 primarily dealt with self-discipline, individual restraint and self-government. The secondary definition of government in 1828 dealt with other spheres of life. The family, management of children, the household and the community were listed. Only last did the old Webster's Dictionary get to civil affairs.

The modern definition places an entirely different emphasis on the word "government." The 1982 edition of Webster's New World Dictionary, Second College Edition, defines government as "The exercise of authority over a state, district, institution, etc." The word "government" has moved from being applied to personal life to being applied to institutional life. As a matter of fact, this later edition of the dictionary makes no mention of personal restraint or self-discipline in any way.

Our thinking has taken us away from where it should be. Our emphasis and responsibility to govern should start with ourselves and work outward. Today, government is a complex institution which may place its own interests over those of the individual. Civil government must not presume responsibility for the salvation of the nation. Salvation comes from God. God expects us to start government within ourselves. However, He places national authorities over us so that the gospel can be advanced.

> *For rulers hold no terror to those who do right, but for those who do wrong. Do you want to be free from fear of the one in authority? Then do what is right and he will commend you. For he is God's servant to do you good. But if you do wrong be afraid, for he does not bear the sword for nothing. He is God's servant, and agent of wrath, to bring punishment to the wrongdoer.*
>
> Romans 13:3-4

The nations are in place so that the issue of the sinfulness of man can be kept under control. If sin were to be allowed to run rampant without restraint, then the nation would not survive. How can the gospel be preached in the midst of anarchy? The judicial system and the courts of justice are designed to restrain evil and preserve order. It preserves the peace to allow for the effective proclamation of the gospel of the Kingdom of God.

The Point of No Return

Why does God save one nation and judges another? What's the difference? There is, what I call, the point of no return for a nation. Have you ever wondered why God allowed Israel to go into Canaan and sometimes said to destroy all those who lived there? He selected some to be totally wiped out while others were allowed to live with restraints. It may be difficult to figure out why God would destroy Sodom and yet save Nineveh.

God may decide to demonstrate His judgment in a nation that is being ripped apart by occultic spirits, sexual perversion and diseases like AIDS that are a judgment upon a people. It would be an act of God's mercy for Him to bring an earthquake and quickly finish the job rather than allow sexual perversion to slowly undermine and destroy a people.

When a nation reaches a point where the community no longer serves as a context within which its citizens can hear and respond to the gospel, that nation has violated its purpose for existence. God does a nation and its people a favor by quick destruction rather than leaving it to gradually and painfully destroy itself.

My experience with civil governments has caused me to believe that the nations are strangling themselves with bureaucracy. All the power seems to have been deposited in the central office and the political capital. Nations have usurped the governments of the family, the workplace, the community, the individual and the Church. In most cases it wasn't done by force. We voted our power over to others because we didn't want to take responsibility ourselves.

So often we are governed and ruled by an institutional agency that is impersonal. It seems to be a large monolithic structure that constantly demands more. Taxes multiply simply to maintain the government, let alone return benefit to the citizens. The bureaucracy of any nation, and the people required to maintain it, extracts the single largest expenditure of most governments. No wonder taxes are so high. God told the Israelites to give ten percent of their income. Most governments take more than a third in income tax alone, with numerous other taxes added.

For the most part, the Church has left the authority and the influencing of the nation up to the politicians. Because the structure of rulership is not rooted in the biblical principles of government, the nation has sidestepped the law of God and established its own statutes and laws based not on God's absolute Word, but on the humanistic thoughts of men. The biblical principles of holiness, righteousness and the morality of God are gradually being eroded from the laws of our nations. Laws have been made which are based only on the intents, passions, desires, ideologies and philosophies of men. With the mistaken notion *vox papuli vox DEI,* these laws are at best vain. Often, I believe, these laws become oppressive and demonic.

God's purpose for the nations is being threatened. When its purpose is threatened and frustrated, that nation will ultimately become degenerate, evil, wicked and immoral. When that wicked nation longs for the supernatural, it invariably will become superstitious and embrace the occult. It inevitably spirals downward, ultimately to destruction.

Again, God will destroy any nation when it reaches the point where the gospel has no currency. That nation has lost its purpose. God will be forced to destroy the nation in order to save the people. God is not committed to structures and offices. He is committed to people. He is committed to people of destiny who will follow His direction. He's committed to a destiny that will bring those who survive into a place where believers will rule the world.

Romans chapter thirteen provides a clear distinction between the rulers of the church and of the state. The Church must provide the ministry of the Word of God with its power to discipline, bless and minister grace to the people. The state must administer social order and justice and serve the purposes of God. If the state usurps power, then the Church has a responsibility to challenge it with a prophetic word of God's judgment.

That destiny will never happen until Jesus comes, because you can't have a perfect world without a perfect leader. In the meantime, we are to occupy until He comes. We must stand firm and possess until He comes. The Church has the task of serving as God's Temple to preserve the nations. He's coming back, and until then we are His Body. Join me now as we look at how the Church must effectively be a kingdom of priests until He returns.

Chapter Seven

Discipling the Nations

The Inadequate Church

Today we might characterize the Church in many different ways. Sometimes a church looks not much better than an entertainment hall, a theater—a place where men only act out a reality without being real themselves. Leaders are on a stage. They respond to the applause of men.

Sometimes a church is little better than a sports stadium, where those who work and train hard are performing well, but only to an audience that takes part vicariously. They feel a part of the success of those who win and the defeat of those who lose, but they are never truly part of the race.

Often a church is little better than a social club where men and women come together to pat each other on the back and to commend one another for their good deeds and for the positions that they hold.

Many churches are like a pity party with men and women who are failures in the world, but who gather together in order to weep on one another's shoulders. Maybe they gather to hide from the world of which they are so afraid.

Do any of these describe your church?

Perhaps your church can be described as an air base, where men and women have their bags already packed and are waiting in the lounge for their chariot to come and take them away. They want to escape from the city, from the world and from humanity. They are waiting to be raptured from a world that is ruptured, battered, beaten and broken.

If you think the world is under judgment, don't forget that judgment begins in the house of the Lord. The next time you walk the street and see prostitutes and drug addicts, or when next you peek into a bar and see men and women drinking themselves into oblivion, remember them. They are crying out for an answer! The whole world is crying for direction. In this respect, the Church is under the judgment of the world. I believe the people we fail to lift up from the ground may one day put us under it.

The opportunity is great, but I fear that the Church of Jesus Christ might reach a point of marginality and of irrelevance. If it abdicates its responsibility, it will become little better than an anachronistic entity.

But there is hope. God is filling His people with a hunger and a thirst after righteousness. There are cities in which Christians are awakening to their divine responsibility to disciple whole nations. It is beginning with an urgent cry among Christians for victory in the face of defeat.

The people of God are now realizing that the world is taking too long to break up and that God is taking even longer to rescue the Church than they imagined. Therefore, the Church is beginning to cry out to Almighty God that it might be restored as a viable, living community.

Discipling the Nation

We are confronted with a world that is falling apart. It will never change until the Church becomes the Church. None of those descriptions that I used to characterize the churches today describe a people who are equipped or willing to change the world. Indeed, the Church is being discipled by the world when it ought to be discipling the world. But how can we disciple the world?

1. Evangelize Nations of Individuals

We are instructed by the Lord that we must disciple the nations. "Therefore go and make disciples of all nations" (Matthew 28:19a). To disciple a nation does not necessarily demand that you become the prime minister or president. Let us not confuse our role of influence in the nation with that of the rule of central government. Jesus was not interested in Herod's office. Nor was He interested in the imperial throne of Caesar. Jesus had authority from His Father. He moved among people where He could effect the most change. He started with influencing individuals.

You can take the nation by capturing the people. If the leaders will not listen, take the message to the people. Share the gospel of Jesus Christ. Teach people how to make Him Lord through following the principles and statutes of God's Word. Give the nation an opportunity to come to the altar and fall down before the Lord God. Teach the true government of God in the homes, schools, work places and the streets.

If you want to understand where true government begins, read Proverbs 25:28: "like a city whose walls are broken down is a man who lacks self-control." In other words, one who has self control is like a strong, impregnable city. That is what we're after when we disciple a nation. We are looking to build up individuals into the kind of people God wants them to be. Self-disciplined individuals under the rule of God create an ordered community.

We are the light of the world. Never take pride in the darkness of your nation. Always spread the light. We are the salt of the earth. We are here to preserve it so that its inhabitants can be saved before Jesus returns. The nation will tread upon the Church if the Church doesn't save the nation.

When Jesus returns, He will bring the angels with Him. They will gather the people together. Some have thought that He will gather the Church. However, according to Matthew 25:32, "All the nations will be gathered before Him." He will gather the nations and select those who inherit eternal life. He will separate the sheep from the goats, the worthy from the unworthy. He will judge the nations. The sheep will enter into joy. The goats will be damned.

Knowing the ultimate destiny of the nations to enter judgment causes me to accept the challenge to evangelize the nations to win individuals.

2. Begin in Jerusalem

The great commission is given to us today, "Go into all the world." Where should we begin? Start at Jerusalem, the home base. Begin where you are and work out from there. Take your community. The problem with us today is that the churches do not identify themselves with the regions they occupy. The church today is not called the way God wants to label His people.

One church where I preached recently is called Faith Revival Ministries. That is a good name. The people of that church know what they are committed to doing. They want to make sure that there is faith, that there is revival and that there is ministry. Certainly nothing can be wrong with that. Our church is called Covenant Community Church. So we fight to make sure members live in covenant and that they recognize their commitment to the community in which they are placed.

Whether we are Baptist, Roman Catholic, Church of God, etc., we spend all of our time defending our theological name, our ritualistic practices and our traditional denominational positions.

Perhaps if we name our churches after the location God has given us to reach we would have more of a vision to actually transform that region. You would be walking around claiming everything in sight. You may want to rename your church like they named them in the first century. There was the church at Ephesus, the church in Galatia, the church of Smyrna, the church of

Philadelphia, and so on. Those churches were identified with their land and with their city. When anybody came to a church, they would know that here is a people to whom God has given a vision for a specific geographic sphere of influence. Where is your Jerusalem?

Our vision is too small. Christ never promised us that we would get the church property as our inheritance. He said, "I'll give you the heathen for your inheritance." He didn't say, "I'll give you the streets where you live." He said, "I'll give you the ends of the earth for your possession." How big is your vision? Do not be crippled or constrained. We have made ourselves midgets in the nations and have allowed the giants out there to confound us. Everything in the world, everything in the earth, everything that belongs to God, belongs to His children. But you must begin in your Jerusalem. You do not qualify to inherit the earth until you have taken care of your local garden.

3. Claim the Nation as Your Own

Who owns your nation? If a church claims a nation as its own, it will more readily assume its responsibility to make disciples of that nation. If we make disciples of the nations, then we will take care of the individuals. Our problem is that we are allowing the nations to gobble up our people, to destroy them and tie them up in hell. God has called the Church to preserve the nations long enough to reach the people with the message of salvation.

Someone once asked, "Why polish brass on a sinking ship?" What are you going to do, sing a hymn while the ship goes down? Will you wait for the helicopter to take you up? Not me! I'm going to look for the leak in the ship. I plan to plug it. I want to fix it. Some may say that I would be working against God if I tried to save the nation. On the contrary, I'm following God's direction to keep the nations afloat long enough to see that a few more get saved. A ship should never be destroyed because of our neglect. Neither should a nation.

4. Pull Down Sprritual Strongholds

Let us intensify our intercession for the nation as a kingdom of priests. Over every nation there is a stronghold. Through his devious dark means, satan has set his own minions all around cities, towns and communities. They are there to do his bidding. It is only through prayer that we can pull down the strongholds of the enemy. The prince of Persia and the prince of Greece are spiritual forces against those cities of God (Daniel 10:20). We can pull them down.

> For our struggle is not against flesh and blood, but against the rulers, against the authorities, against the powers of this dark world and against the spiritual forces of evil in the heavenly realms...And pray in the Spirit on all occasions with all kinds of prayers and requests. With this in mind be alert and always keep on praying for all the saints.
>
> Ephesians 6:12,18

Every year fortune-telling seems to flourish just before a new year begins. The end-of-the-year newspapers are filled with it. They make predictions about what will happen and what we're looking forward to in the year to come. People are becoming famous for their predictions. The Lord abhors the occult (Isaiah 47:11-15). We need to take authority against it in prayer and turn the people's attention toward faith in God.

We're targeting things when we pray. We realize that the land belongs to us more than it belongs to any politician, businessman, social worker or anyone who is not part of God's Kingdom. Intercede for your own nation.

I urge then, first of all, that requests, prayers, interces-sion, and thanksgiving be made for everyone—for kings and all those in authority, that we may live peaceful and quiet lives in all godliness and holiness. This is good and pleases God our Savior who wants all men to be saved and to come to a knowledge of the truth.

1 Timothy 2:1-3

Paul is speaking to Timothy and the Church when he says that we've got to pray and intercede, giving thanks for everyone. First of all we pray for those in authority. Pray for kings. For Paul to highlight kings implies that he must have the nation in mind because an authority cannot exist without a government in which to function. Pray for your nation, insuring that those in authority are kept before the throne of God. Why? So that we may live peaceful and quiet lives in all godliness and holiness.

The quality of life in the nation is in direct propor-tion to the faithful prayers of the saints of God. God is after something. He's not talking about individuals here.

He's talking about an entire nation, a people, a culture, a society, a community.

5. Purify Yourself

The only way for the Church to have any hope of victory in the midst of a perverse world is to purify itself. Judgment begins first in the house of the Lord. This was God's promise to Solomon.

The temple was just finished being built and Solomon was giving thanks and praising God, seeking to have the assurance from God of His faithful protection and provision for Israel. Solomon spent time in prayer. He spent a whole night in prayer. He summoned the people together to celebrate and offer sacrifices before God. Then these verses pick up the story.

> *"...I have heard your prayer and have chosen this place for Myself as a temple for sacrifices. When I shut up the heavens so that there is no rain, or command locusts to devour the land or send a plague among My people, if My people, who are called by My name, will humble themselves and pray and seek My face and turn from their wicked ways, then will I hear from heaven and will forgive their sin and will heal their land. Now My eyes will be open and My ears attentive to the prayers offered in this place.*

2 Chronicles 7:12-15

Can these verses be made relevant to our time? Let's examine the passage carefully. It's good to know that God hears our prayers. A king's prayer ought to be heard. He's very important, isn't he? We are kings too, aren't we? That's one of the most reassuring things to know after you've labored in prayer to get an assurance from God that He hears your prayers.

Do you know that God shuts up the heavens? Do you know that God brings drought? In Jamaica we had an interesting debate following the devastation of Hurricane Gilbert. Was Gilbert sent by the devil or by God? This passage makes it clear, God is sovereign over nature. God does shut up the heavens and He opens the heavens. Locusts come to devour the land. It is God who commands them.

Regardless of what calamities come upon a nation, He sends strength among His people. Can the Church claim the same promises made to Israel in this passage? Surely, if we are His people, called by His name, and if we pray, seek His face and turn from our wicked ways, He will hear from Heaven and heal our land. The Church must first deal with its own sins before God will heal its nations. In the Old Testament, the priests purified themselves before they bore the iniquity of the nation. The nations will never see God until they can look through the transparency of the Church, the dwelling place of God.

6. Stand in the Gap

God is looking for a people who will stand in the gap for their nation. This is what Moses did when he made atonement for the rebellious people in the wilderness.

When the people saw that Moses was so long in coming down from the mountain, they gathered around Aaron and said, "Come, make us gods who will go before us. As for this fellow Moses who brought us up out of Egypt, we don't know what has happened to him." Aaron answered them, "Take off the gold earrings that your wives, your sons, and your daughters are wearing, and bring them to me." So all the people took off their earrings and brought them to Aaron. He took what they handed him and made it into an idol cast in the shape of a calf, fashioning it with a tool. Then they said, "These are your gods O Israel, who brought you up out of Egypt."

Exodus 32:1-4

Their sin was great. The idea that they could worship a golden calf and attribute the works of God to it was preposterous. However, they fell into pagan worship, which angered God. The Lord was so displeased that He planned to destroy them instantly. The entire nation would have died immediately in the desert if it were not for Moses. Moses stood in the gap on their behalf. "But now, please forgive their sin—but if not, then blot me out of the book you have written" (Exodus 32:32). God listened to the prayers of Moses and allowed the nation to survive.

Our world is full of many idols. Some people worship fame and fortune. Others worship at the altars of self-gratification. Still others are bold enough to openly worship demons and call them god. No matter how deep into sin a nation falls, the Church can pray on behalf of the land and God will hear. He would have spared Sodom for only ten righteous people. How much more so will He listen to His Church today.

It is our first responsibility to be identified as a kingdom of priests. The only way to make disciples of the nations is to start on our knees in prayer. The battle will be won when believers begin to pray the way they should.

7. Govern Self and the Family

How am I to be governed? Government begins with the discipline of self. If I am properly governed, then I will look after my family. The drug problem is not going to be solved by parliaments and politicians. It is going to be solved in the family. If my wife and I manage our home correctly, and care for our children, then they will not feel rejected. They will not feel bored with life. They will not be looking for a "high," or for love somewhere else. They will find it under the discipline and government of our home. Therefore, I would have solved the problems of society for those in my household. All the problems of the nations—immorality, occult, corruption, crime, taxes and self-gratification—will be solved as God's people begin to govern themselves properly.

8. Decentralize Power

Another step in preserving the nations is for the Church to begin to decentralize power. The previous chapter explained how the concept of government has changed and how we have given our personal responsibilities over to a complex civil bureaucracy. Unless we decentralize government, the seat of power and control will succumb to corruption.

In the Church it is good strategy to establish cell groups within each community. Cell groups must become the center of life for each area. They must become the salt for the different neighborhoods. You can evangelize more personally and effectively in your small community through personal witness, visitation and social interaction. You can pray for specific, relevant needs. You can tear down evil principalities and powers which affect your community's government and oppress the people both locally and nationally. The church in the local community can insure proper rule and administration within schools, community clubs and other local institutions by providing responsible leaders to function in those spheres.

Most social issues need to be dealt with at the local level. I have already mentioned how a family solves its social problems. The community is an extension of the family, or groups of families. Some things are too big for one family to have the resources to solve. Therefore, we must band together into communities to confront the problem.

Do you understand why God chided the people when they asked for a king? The problem was not the fact that they asked for a king. The problem was what would happen when power was vested in a central government. The king became an institution himself, and the people became enslaved to the government.

But when they said, "Give us a king to lead us," this displeased Samuel, so he prayed to the Lord. And the Lord told him, "Listen to all that the people are saying to you; it is not you they have rejected, but they have rejected Me as their king...Now listen to them; but warn them solemnly and let them know what the king who will reign over them will do."

1 Samuel 8:6-7,9

There is nothing wrong with having a central government with a king, prime minister or president. Genuine central government works for the benefit of the local communities rather than for the benefit of itself. The central government is there to protect the rights of the people and to put constraints on those who would do evil.

The Bible tells us that righteousness exalts a nation. We've got to understand that God has a word for the nation that will judge the nation. The Scriptures are not exclusivly for the Church, with another book of philosophy for the nation. God is looking for nations that will be characterized in their cultures, their attitudes, their morals and their ethics by the Word of God.

9. Impact the Culture

God is looking in nations for values and attitudes to be righteous. Once again in First Timothy Paul writes, "This is good, and pleases God our Savior, who wants all men to be saved and to come to a knowledge of the truth" (1 Timothy 2:3). Surely He wants a quality of life to dominate and characterize your nation so that individuals might be saved.

The culture of a people is the collective expression of that people. We must impact the culture of our nations. Culture is that which is built upon the natural. Water is natural, but a canal is cultural. The wood from the tree is natural, but the house built with the wood is cultural. Sound and rhythm are natural, but Reggae is cultural.

Who determines the culture of a nation? The people of God must work to redeem and establish the culture of their nations. The Church is often influenced by culture. God wants us to be the influencer. We must raise the culture to God's standards rather than allow the Church to be reduced by atheistic and humanistic values. Our culture must not only remind us of our past, it must also take us into the future.

Culture must not be based merely on a description of the present; it must be determinative and tied to destiny. Our plays and our songs must not simply reflect what is, but must speak to what ought to be. I'm longing to see the theater and stage filled with dramatic presentations of a vision for destiny. Are we there yet? I am longing to see God's plan fulfilled. We must produce cultural material that will permit God to fashion us according to what He wants us to become.

I believe that we need a new dimension to our culture that is creative and visionary. When men and women listen to the songs and watch the movies of these creative visionaries, they should see what God wants to do. Even our buildings and edifices should reflect a vision of God. Culture needs to be a positive, enduring influence on the nation.

If the nation disintegrates, if violence and greed take over, if you're persecuted, let it not be because you did not help the nation. Let us not allow the destruction of our people to occur because we neglected to influence the culture of our land. Let it be because the world was pressed in by your challenge and they rebelled against it. They will rebel. But give them a chance to do so.

How many Christians today are persecuted? Very few. Jesus told His disciples that believers are to be different from the world's systems and culture.

> *"Do not suppose that I have come to bring peace to the earth. I did not come to bring peace, but a sword. For I have come to turn 'a man against his father, a daughter against her mother, a daughter-in-law against her mother-in-law—a man's enemies will be the members of his own household.' "*

Matthew 10:34-36

How can it be that the church today faces very little persecution and opposition? Perhaps it is because we have been too much like the worldly culture of our nations, because no one can tell we are different. God's people are to influence the culture of their nations, and that influence will not be without opposition.

Much of the world's culture stands in total opposition to the principles of Christianity. The world is selfish and lustful. Its culture is constantly raising up the ideal of materialism and greed. Christianity is based upon a God of love. Love is the exact opposite of lust. Love gives; lust takes. Certainly there should be a clash of values within the culture of our nations.

God desires us to have a quality life that stems from sacrificial love for one another. Jesus said, "A new command I give you: Love one another, as I have loved you, so you must love one another. By this all men will know that you are My disciples, if you love one another" (John 13:34-35). The selfishness displayed in the culture of the nations must be challenged by the influence of the Church toward a self-sacrificing love.

The Church of Jesus Christ is called to disciple the nations. How can we make disciples? We pray and intercede as God's priests in the nation. Then we proclaim the truth throughout the land as God's prophets and evangelists. As kings, the saints must exercise rulership within a decentralized state and establish a counterculture in keeping with the principles of the Word of God.

Chapter Eight

Establishing Your Nation

Does God Save a Nation?

When I was a youngster growing up, I was taught to love Jamaica. I was born there and I loved the people. I was made to have a sense of national pride. Yet when I became a Christian, I wasn't quite so sure what my attitude should be toward the nation. When you grow up in the evangelical or Pentecostal circles, you are taught so much about the world to come that you're not so sure what God thinks about this present world. The question came to me in the midst of problems and difficulties, "Does God save a nation?" I was convinced that God was interested in individuals, but what about a nation? If He saved me as an individual, would He also save a nation?

Sometimes when we speak with great solicitude about our country I sense concern in the faces of the people. They may be thinking, "Why doesn't the pastor just consider my problems and personal needs, difficulties and frustrations? Why is he always concerning himself about the community? Does God save a nation?" Surely my name is written in the Lamb's Book of Life. I'm looking forward to seeing Jesus face to face. Yet will there be a corner with a plaque on it that says, "Jamaica?" Or "Trinidad and Tobago?" Or "United States of America?" I'll make it there, but does God save a nation?

I'm challenging you to consider this question because, deep down within our own hearts, in our minds, we are sometimes afraid to cause these questions to surface. We're brought up with traditional ideas. We're challenged to be religious. We're sometimes more concerned about what the preacher thinks than what the Word says. But deep down you may be asking the question, "Does God save a nation?"

I'm concerned about the nations because I believe the nations have no future without the Church. In the end-time there will be triumph. The Church is not going out secretly as some weak, feeble, failing entity. God intends for us to take hold of the nations.

The time is coming when the leaders in civil government, business, education, recreation, entertainment, health and justice will come to men of God for solutions to the problems they face. Pharaoh found a man with the Spirit of God and made him ruler of all Egypt when he knew he faced devastation (Genesis 41:38). The nations will look to believers when believers become equipped with the wisdom of the Word for our times. They will embrace us. They will see the viable solutions we have to offer from God's Word. Believing wise men will receive votes and be placed in office, not through militant power struggles, but because the wisdom of God's people will become obvious.

There will be a shift from the empty leadership of central government to the resourcefulness of the "Nation" within a nation. I'm referring to the holy nation—the Church. The Church will be filled with the resources of wisdom, understanding and knowledge. Christians will have the strength, the courage and the determination to lead their nations. Eventually there will be a clash of authorities. But God's purpose for the nations will be determined by the people of God.

A Spiritual Word to the Islands of the Sea

God speaks to us a word from Isaiah 43, verses 18 through 21. This is a message that jumps out of the pages of the Scriptures and runs through the passage of time, meeting us head-on in our time, in our nation. It causes a word written centuries ago to be a word alive for us today. It is a word of hope in a time of despair. And He says to us today, as He said in the times of Isaiah:

Forget the former things; do not dwell on the past.
See, I am doing a new thing!
Now it springs up; do you not perceive it?
I am making a way in the desert and streams in the wasteland.
The wild animals honor Me, the jackals and the owls,
because I provide water in the desert and streams in the wasteland,

to give drink to My people, My chosen,
the people I formed for Myself that they may proclaim
*   My praise.*

Today more than ever, we need to hear a word of hope. We need to hear some good news. We strain our ears to hear a new word as we recognize that our hearts are hungry and thirsty for the living Word of God to spring forth before us and to give us a new lease on life. We have such a God, who is not at a loss to give us a word of hope, a new way, a new word, and to usher in a new day. We have a God who is willing, able and available to give to us the Word of life. We look to this God, who is the Lord God Almighty, and we see Him as the source of all might, power and hope. As Christians, we have the responsibility to bring this word of hope to our island nations in our time.

The best news the world can pluck out of the events of our time with which to mark the headlines that startle us each morning is bad news—words of despair, words of frustration, words of discouragement. Where is the hope for our time and for our nation? We cannot live without hope. We need good news. We need the gospel of hope!

What Is Hope?

I believe this is a question that is going over in your mind. What is hope? Well, hope is not an expression of wishful thinking. It is not an expression of doubt. It is not an expression of anxiety and fear. Hope is not an expression of chance or of luck, but that is how we use it, for that is what the world has taught us concerning hope in our time.

But there is another hope that God has given us, and God has so made us that we cannot live without hope. Without hope, we cannot face tomorrow. Hope is a confident expectation about the future. It is an expectation that is saying, "I know what tomorrow holds." It is an expectation that is based on faith and on a strong and firm belief in the future. Therefore, if hope is based on faith, then we have to be careful in what we place our faith because faith is something that we believe now, that gives us hope for tomorrow. If you have no faith today, then you cannot have hope for tomorrow.

Misplaced Faith—False Hope

The Bible says, "Faith is the substance of things hoped for...." It is important for you to realize that *if your faith is in the wrong place, then you are living under a false hope*. Today we have misplaced our faith. We have been a people of misplaced faith and therefore we have been a people of false hope.

Through the pains of slavery, through the period of indentured labor and through the time of self-government and into independence, regardless of what has been recorded for us by men who do not know God, we can see that the hand of God has been at work amongst our people. He has taught us to look beyond the pains of slavery and to see the God of our hope. We sometimes criticize the old choruses which speak of "a pie in the sky by and by." However, there was no pie on earth for the people in the times of slavery. If they did not see that the heavens were open and that God had a large pie in the sky for them, they would have lived without any hope. Our people would have died out in slavery in the same way that the indigenous Indians died out many centuries ago at the hands of the colonists. But, thank God for those who came from Europe. We may say that they came and exploited us, but in those same merchant ships God sent missionaries with the Word of God to bring us the word of salvation so that we as a people learned the songs of God. We sang the songs of God and God taught us to look to Him. As a result, we became a people of God.

But we have run up against a problem. We have fought for independence—independence from Europe—but in doing so we have unintentionally struggled for independence from God, much to our loss. God says to us through the writings of the prophet Jeremiah:

> *My people have committed two sins. They have forsaken Me, the spring of living water and have dug out their own cisterns, broken cisterns that cannot hold water.*
>
> Jeremiah 2:13

As nations we have misplaced our faith, so whatever hope we thought we had was a false hope.

Ways in which We Have Misplaced Our Faith

You might ask, "How have we misplaced our faith?" Let us look at three ways in which we have committed this sin:

1. First, we have tended to look to national leaders. If you think of the period of time from the 40's to our own present time, you will notice that all the men who rose to prominence in our lands did so because we saw them as messiahs or as saviors. They have even gone as far as to take on biblical names and to assume personalities and characteristics that would make them look like gods among us. They are not to be blamed. The blame is ours.

   We have almost deified our leaders, just as we have deified our national heroes. We have put our faith in their good qualities without recognizing that they also have weaknesses. So when we lifted them up on a pedestal, we did not realize that their weaknesses would have brought them down. Now their failures strike us in the face and smash our hopes. All this happens because we misplaced our faith, and we have now turned around to destroy the very men that we built up.

   God says, "I will not give My glory to another." We have placed extraordinary faith in ordinary men, and so we have built false hopes in them. We are now reaping the results of it. We have only ourselves to blame. We should honor our leaders. However, we must be cautious in our actions. Let men be men and let God be God.

2. Secondly, we have misplaced our faith in these days in material things. We have never really been wealthy islands, but I believe that we have always had sufficient

in material resources—bananas, bauxite, oil, the beauty of our land. But these things have led us to seek after more and more material things and to misplace our faith as if our hope has its source in the things we possess. A spirit of acquisitiveness has really taken hold of us as nations.

We measure our prestige by whether we have a car, whether we have some land or the kind of house in which we live. We invested more in these things than we have in our own sons and daughters. All of us are guilty, whether rich or poor, whether employers or employees, whether in the management sector or in the labor sector. We are all guilty of this sin.

We need to begin to see where we must place our faith and then fight the battle from the right perspectives. Jesus Christ well said, "You cannot serve God and mammon."

If our material resources are to work for our good rather than for our destruction, we have to look beyond bananas and bauxite, beyond oil and the beauty of the land. We need to look to God Himself. If we fail to reach that point, then we will still have our faith misplaced and our hope false.

3. A third area in which we have misplaced our faith is in plans and programs, in ideas and ideologies. Let's think back over our recent history. We have been "suckers." We have been sucked in by one program after another. We have given way to one set of ideas

after another. We have followed one dream after another.

We have tried every ideology. We have flirted with every block and model—the Western block, the Eastern block, the Cuban model, the Puerto Rican model, the Russian model. Are we going back to Africa, or are we going to create a Third World?

God wants to warn us, as a nation, that we should be careful of following any program adopting any plan, becoming part of any ideology or being sucked into any kind of "ism" that does not make room for God.

These programs have caught our fancy because they seem ideal. An ideal is good, since it presents a hope and gives us direction. It even motivates us. However, these programs are based only on humanism and materialism. They are rooted in the ability of atonymous man.

No man should attempt to lead his nation who is not himself led by God. The leader is more important than the institution, and the individual more important than the program. I would much rather be led by a person than by a program. It may be the best program in the world, but if the person behind it is not a righteous man, then there is no guarantee that that program will be carried through. On the other hand the program may not look good, but if the man is a man of God, then he will be available to be used by God moment by moment, every day of the year.

The Bible says, "When the righteous are in authority, the people rejoice; but when the wicked beareth rule, the people mourn" (Proverbs 29:2, KJV). Proverbs 11:11 says, "The good influence of godly citizens causes a city to prosper..." (LB). Proverbs 25:19 warns us, "Putting confidence in an unreliable man is like chewing with a sore tooth, or trying to run on a broken foot" (LB).

Be careful where you place your faith, and be sure to place it where God can take hold of it and make it fulfill your hopes.

The Basis of Our Hope

What then is the basis of our hope in our time? I want to mention three things:

1. Our hope is faith in the Sovereignty of God.

    If God is not ruling, and if God is not in control, then I have no hope whatsoever.

    If Jesus Christ could not have said, "Thy Kingdom come on earth as it is in heaven," then I would have no hope whatsoever.

    If Jesus Christ never said, "All power is given unto Me in heaven and on earth," then I would have no hope whatsoever.

    If the Psalmist could not cry out, "The Lord has established His throne and His kingdom rules over all," then I would have no hope whatsoever.

    If I could not look forward in the future and say, "The kingdom of the world has become the

Kingdom of our Lord and of His Christ, and
He shall reign for ever and ever," then I would
have no hope whatsoever.
If I did not know that God fashions our history,
then I might as well die today,
Because I would be without hope.

David praised the Lord in the presence of the whole as-
sembly, saying, "Praise be to you, O Lord, God of our
father Israel, from everlasting to everlasting. Yours, O
Lord, is the greatness and the power and the glory and
the majesty and the splendor, for everything in Heaven
and earth is yours. Yours, O Lord, is the Kingdom; you
are exalted as head over all.

1 Chronicles 29:10-11

We need to know that the Sovereign Lord is in control.

He is in control of the heavens,
And He is in control of the earth;
He rules in the heavens,
And He rules in the affairs of men.
We say, Lord God Almighty, 'El Shaddai',
Supreme God, Sovereign Lord,
The God of Gods, the King of Kings, the Lord
of Lords, Immortal, Immovable,
Omnipotent, the Holy God who lives in the high
and lofty place.
All authority and power belong to Him:
All riches belong to Him, and He rules on earth.

Unless you reach the point where you can put your faith in Almighty God, then you are misplacing your faith in this land. Unless you first find faith in God, your placing your faith in men makes no sense. It is a good thing to be able to have faith in men, but only after you have placed faith in your God above men.

2. The basis of our new hope is faith in God's covenant promise to us in the islands of the sea.

By covenant, I mean an agreement that God has made—a commitment that He will never break. In Psalm 89:33-34, God says through the Psalmist:

> ...*I will not take My love from him, nor will I ever betray My faithfulness.*
> *I will not violate My covenant or alter what My lips have uttered.*

God is simply saying this: "My faithfulness will never fail and My covenant I will never break." If God has said so, it shall be so. His word will never return empty, but it will accomplish that which He has purposed. He is a covenant God who does not know what it is to break a promise. If God has spoken to us, you can be very sure that He is going to send His Holy Spirit to ensure that the Word of God is accomplished.

In these days, we not only have been reading the Word of God, but we also have been listening to the current word of God as it comes to us by the Holy Spirit. At times it comes by prophecy, at times by a word of revelation, sometimes by the preached word, and sometimes by vision, tongues and interpretation. This is the current word of God coming on the wings of the Spirit of God, especially for us in our time, in our land.

Has God spoken to your nation? God deals covenantally with nations. Perhaps you did not realize it, but God nurtures us from infancy until we recognize Him (Hosea 11). Take Jamaica, for example. It wasn't until the time that we lowered the flag of the British Union Jack, raised our own flag and stood with our hands firm and with due honor and awe before Almighty God, that we raised our heads and finally recognized Him to be "Our Father." This pleased Him as we sang our national anthem:

> Eternal Father, bless our land,
> Guard us with Thy mighty hand,
> Keep us free from evil powers,
> Be our light through countless hours.
> To our leaders, Great Defender,
> Grant true wisdom from above.
> Justice, truth be ours forever,
> Jamaica, land we love.
> Jamaica, Jamaica, Jamaica land we love.
>
> Teach us true respect for all,
> Stir response to duty's call,
> Strengthen us the weak to cherish,
> Give us vision lest we perish.
> Knowledge send us heavenly Father,
> Grant true wisdom from above.

Justice, truth be ours forever,
Jamaica, land we love.
Jamaica, Jamaica, Jamaica land we love.

That was our commitment to God. I believe God took us seriously and that is what is saving us today. Although we have turned our backs upon God, He still hears the echoing sound of our voices as we sing it time and time again, against the walls of the National Arena, against the walls of our churches and against the walls of our meeting places as we gather as a nation and as a people. It is a word of confidence that God is determined to see us as a people with whom He will keep His side of the bargain. He is a covenant God, and we are His covenant people.

This may be the same with your nation. God's covenant may be reflected in your name, your motto, your constitution, your national pledge or prayer or some other national symbol. You must take it seriously.

God gave a word by prophecy, through our sister Babsie Bleasdell of Trinidad in 1977. This is a word for the whole Caribbean area:

"The living waters of My Spirit flood this land
To mingle with the waters of the Caribbean.
Oh, My people, says God—
How I long to draw you to Myself.

"I brought you from many nations
To create of you ONE PEOPLE.
You are My covenant people of the

twentieth century.
My heart delights as I see
Men of the Caribbean pass by—
Of many hues, of many colors,
Of many persuasions—
All made one in Me;
For I am the Lord.
I long to heal your nostrils
Of the smell of the slave ships,
Says God.
I long to heal your ears
From the crack of the slave driver's whip;
I long to heal you
In the deep recesses of your heart.
I long to make you whole,
To make you My people—
A people of whom I can be very proud;
That you may know Me as God.
And I shall bring men from nations across the sea
To see men of the Caribbean pass by—
MY PEOPLE.
And they shall know that I am God
And I alone could do this thing—
Weave many races into one people,
And make men of all colors, a people,
An holy people, a people of God.
Then God said to us—
I could not say to many of you,
"Let your elders be pure and holy;
For your elders have all been tainted.
But I long to heal you

117

From the shame of your bastardy.
I want to wash your faces clean
And I want to make you holy.
So, out of the Magdalens and the Zacheusses,
I shall raise up My people;
And all will know that I am God
And that I dwell with My people—
Says the Lord."

3. We have new hope when we make a faith response to God through Jesus Christ.

This faith response, on a personal and national basis involves at least two things:
   (i)   Repentance
   (ii) Obedience
Every citizen must have an opportunity to hear the gospel and to respond to it. The basic information is simple.

(1) Recognize you are a sinner. "*All* have sinned and come short of the glory of God" (Romans 3:23).

(2) Sin is destructive to your entire life. "The wages of sin is death" (Romans 6:23).

(3) You cannot rescue yourself. "He saved us not because of righteous things we had done but because of His mercy." (Titus 3:5).

(4) God's solution is the gift of Jesus Christ. "God so loved the world that He gave His only begotten Son." (John 3:16).

(5) Your response is to repent, receive Jesus Christ as your Savior and commit yourself to walk in obedience to His Word both spiritually and ethically.

None of us can come before the face of Almighty God and survive as if we were righteous. When Moses came before the glory of God, he could not stand to see the Shekinah glory. God had to rescue him. He said, "Take your shoes from off your feet, for the place on which you stand is holy ground." When Isaiah was worshiping and praising Almighty God in the temple, he was concerned about the state of his nation. God came before him, and he said, "Woe is me, for I am undone; a man of unclean lips and I dwell amongst a people of unclean lips." When Peter recognized the glory of God in Jesus Christ, he was forced to fall down before Him. And he said, "Lord, have mercy on me, a sinner." When Thomas, through his doubt, saw that Jesus Christ was the living God, he worshiped Him and he bowed down before Him and he said, "My Lord, and my God...."

None of us can feel clean until this entire nation is cleansed. You need to take this step of faith. When we come before God in mourning, repentance and obedience to His Word, it is only then that we will begin to see the despair, the disillusionment and the frustration being rolled back bit by bit. God will then come and pick us up—filthy rags— from off the ground, dust us off and transform us into a robe of righteousness. God desires to cleanse the nation and bring us into prosperity and back to being a people of hope, but not of false hope, and a people of faith, but not of misplaced faith.

In Deuteronomy 28:1-14, the Bible says:

If you fully obey the Lord your God and carefully follow all His commands I give you today, the Lord your God will set you high above all the nations on earth. All these blessings will come upon you and accompany you if you obey the Lord your God:

You will be blessed in the city and blessed in the country. The fruit of your womb will be blessed, and the crops of your land and the young of your livestock—the calves of your herds and the lambs of your flocks. Your basket and your kneading trough will be blessed. You will be blessed when you come in and blessed when you go out.

The Lord will grant that the enemies who rise up against you will be defeated before you. They will come at you from one direction but flee from you in seven. The Lord will send a blessing on your barns and on everything you put your hand to. The Lord your God will bless you in the land He is giving you. The Lord will establish you as His holy people, as He promised you on oath, if you keep the commands of the Lord your God and walk in His ways. Then all the peoples on earth will see that you are called by the name of the Lord, and they will fear you. The Lord will grant you abundant prosperity—in the fruit of your womb, the young of your livestock and the crops of your ground—in the land He swore to your forefathers to give you. The Lord will open the heavens, the storehouse of His bounty, to send rain on your land in season and to bless all the work of your hands. You will lend to many nations but will borrow from none. The Lord will make you the head, not the tail. If you pay attention to the commands of the Lord your God that I give you this day and carefully follow them, you will always be at the top, never at the bottom. Do not turn aside from any of the commands I give you today, to the right or to the left, following other gods and serving them.

These are the blessings that God has for your land. Take this first step by placing your faith in Him. He is the source of all hope.

Join with a friend at home, at school, at the workplace, in the street and commit your nation to God. Be God's Tabernacle in the wilderness, His temple in the city and the Body of Christ among the people. For wherever two or three are gathered together there He is in the midst. *Pray*:

Almighty God, we recognize today that You have nurtured us as a people, in times gone by. But, Lord, in seeking to become an independent people we have struggled because we have sought to be independent of You. We are sorry. Forgive us, O God. We ask You to forgive us of our own sins. Cause us to move in obedience to You. We acknowledge that You are the Sovereign Lord, and today we enthrone You and claim that You are the King and the Lord of this nation and declare Your rulership over the Parliament and over the security forces, and over the business houses, and in every home, and among the masses of the people, among the poor and among the wealthy, among the employers and the employees. We declare Your Sovereign rule, O God. As You rule in the heavens, so rule upon this land. We thank You, O God, that we can have faith in Your Sovereign control and power and we can have faith in Your covenant promise to us as a people. Give us hope, O God, in a time of despair.

Amen

Chapter Highlights

This section contains excerpts from each chapter. Most of them are direct or near quotes.

Each statement can stand on its own as a complete thought. The interested reader may use it as the basis for discussion or for further study.

Chapter One—The Origin of Nations

● The world consists of the earth, its natural resources, governmental systems and structures, and people. To carry out His purposes, God divided this whole world into nations.

● When God establishes a nation, He causes a people to come together from different traditions, languages, and cultures, but He weaves them together as one integrated community.

● God establishes a nation from a common seed. Through this He gives them an ethnic consciousness; then they develop a social contract, then they are identified with their own land; then they become a national political unit. A nation is not a nation unless it is a nation under God.

Chapter Two—Preserving the Purpose and Destiny of Nations

● The people of the world will remain tragically condemned if the people who have been called from out of the world (i.e. the Church), do not understand their purpose in the world.

● The plans of any nation are futile and will come to naught unless they are aligned to God's destiny for that nation. Unfortunately not every nation seeks God's plan.

● A level of corruption, selfish exploitation and rapacious greed pervades our modern societies. Envy, hatred and violence so threatens the security of the community, I wonder whether we could survive a visitation from God to our cities.

● The potential for human accomplishment is beyond our imagination. However, our God-given potential should not arrogate itself to a position of pride.

● Centralized autonomous man always seeks to deify his selfish ambitions and idolize his humanistic achievements.

● The creeping moral degeneracy of our people is leading to a progressive dehumanization of our generation. Permissive sexual promiscuity is giving way to every form of sexual perversion. Personal ungodliness is now so conventional it is becoming culturally, institutionally and legally oppressive.

● Most nations possess an innate sense of being birthed by a determined spirit that is bigger than a purely human agency. It is a divine consciousness of destiny often enshrined in anthems, national pledges and constitutions. Whether it is acknowledged as divine or not, history eventually vindicates the sovereign hand of God in the affairs of men.

Chapter Three—Israel: God's Chosen Nation

● The God of generations whose intention it was to build out of the loins of one man, a great nation, planted His purpose in the seed of Abraham. It was a master stroke.

● God was not after Abraham as a person. He only wanted a servant or an instrument. He was after the nations of the world.

● It was out of His sanctuary of Heaven that God spoke to Noah and to Abraham. But out of the sanctuary of the mountain, He gave directions to Moses.

● Justice, honesty, sexual propriety, ownership of property and all the various civil laws needed for a nation to be civilized where enshrined in the Ten Commandments of Sinai and given to Moses.

Chapter Four— God's Sanctuary in the Nation (Old Testament)

● The Law of God is not designed to elicit blind obedience to rules. What God wants is a relationship with His people. The law exposes unrighteousness, and reveals a gap between a sinful people and a holy God.

● The God of the Sanctuary of Heaven who came down to the sanctuary of the great mountain now had come down in the sanctuary of the tabernacle of meeting. This was structured according to the spiritual tabernacle which is in heaven.

● To whomever you dedicate the firstborn or given the firstfruit, that person is to you "el numero uno".

● The sanctuary became the place of instruction, council and direction...whenever the people wanted to hear from God they would not cry out to the heavens. They would no longer go to the mountain. They would come to the place of appointment—the tabernacle.

● The Church maintains a distinct identity from that of the nation. It is more precise to identify it with the priestly tribe of Levi in the midst of the nation than with the nation of Israel itself.

● The priests of any generation are the firstfruit of their nation. If the firstfruits are holy, the whole nation is sanctified unto God.

● You cannot restore a nation and you cannot change a world until the Church is first changed.

Chapter Five— God's Sanctuary Among the Nations (New Testament)

● The Church has missed the full dimension of the great commission when it only tries to make disciples of individuals.

● We have become the natural Body of Christ connected to its supernatural head who is at the right hand of the Father in Heaven. We are the temple of God among the nations.

● The first step for us as a Church is not to be an army, but to be a sanctuary. The direction the world needs can only come from out of the council of the Ark of the Most Holy Place.

● The tabernacle in the wilderness became the temple in the city. Now the temple in the city has become the Body of Christ, among the peoples of the world.

Chapter Six—The Purpose of the Nations

● Nations are established by God for two purposes: 1.) the whole earth be inhabited by men, and 2.) men will be able to find Him.

● Many Christians see themselves as squatters on the land nervously enduring with grim determination until the Lord returns to rescue them from the threat of the enemy. But God is allowing the nations to watch over His resources in trust until the Church is ready to claim its full inheritance.

● God established nations to be a type of market-place from which Jesus Christ would purchase men with the currency of His blood, to become another nation, a Kingdom of priests.

● Civil government must not presume responsibility for the salvation of the people. Salvation comes from God alone through the agency of His Church.

● When a nation reaches a point that its communities no longer serve as a context within which its citizens can hear and respond to the gospel, that nation has violated its purpose for existence.

● The state must administer social order and justice and serve the purposes of God. If the state usurps power then the Church has a responsibility to challenge it with the prophetic word of God's judgement.

Chapter Seven—Discipling the Nations

● The people you fail to lift up from the ground may one day put you under it.

● I fear that the Church of Jesus Christ has reached a point of marginality and irrelevance. If it abdicates its responsibility it will become little better than an anachronistic entity.

● When the Church claims a nation as its own, it will more readily assume its responsibility to disciple that nation.

● The quality of life in the nation is in direct proportion to the faithful prayers of the saints of God.

● The nation will never see God until it can look through the transparency of the Church, the dwelling place of God.

● The church in the local community can ensure proper rule and administration within schools, clubs and other local institutions by providing responsible leaders to function in those spheres.

● The culture of a people is the collective artistic expression of that people. It must not only remind us of the past or be descriptive of the present, it must be determinative and tied to destiny.

Chapter Eight—Establishing Your Nation

● The nations have no future without the Church. The time is coming when the leaders in civil government, business, education, recreation, entertainment, health, and justice will come to men of God for solutions to the problems they face.

● Hope is a confident expectation about the future. It is based on faith. Therefore, be careful in what you place your faith. Faith is something you believe now, that gives hope for tomorrow.

● No man should lead his people who is not himself led by God.

● We must never follow any person or programme or be sucked into any kind of "ism" that does not make room for God.

● If God's covenant is reflected in your nation through its name, its motto, its constitution, its national pledge, its prayer or some other national symbol—you must take it seriously.

● Every citizen must get an opportunity to hear the gospel and to respond to it.

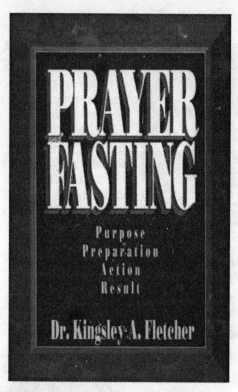

PRAYER AND FASTING by *Kingsley Fletcher.* Satan is having a field day, diverting the attention of God's people away from God. The enemy of our soul is so afraid of our unused power in God that he is trying to confuse us. He wants to keep us from the increased power we receive as we pray and fast. Fasting along with prayer sharpens your expectancy so that when you ask, you expect to receive. Discover the benefits of successful prayer and fasting. TPB-168 p. ISBN 1-56043-070-2 Retail $6.95 **TO ORDER: CALL 1-800-722-6774**